ACCESSING
THE *Scriptures*
THROUGH STUDY AND PRAYER

Believing and Being—More Than a Convert

TWO BIBLE WORK STUDIES
FOR - INDIVIDUALS - COUPLES - GROUPS

THE GENERAL LETTERS OF
HEBREWS, JAMES, PETER,
JOHN, JUDE

JOHN PENNINGTON
LARGE PRINT BIBLE STUDIES
VOLUME II

WESTBOW
PRESS®
A DIVISION OF THOMAS NELSON
& ZONDERVAN

WestBow Press books may be ordered through booksellers or by contacting:

WestBow Press
A Division of Thomas Nelson & Zondervan
1663 Liberty Drive
Bloomington, IN 47403
www.westbowpress.com
1 (866) 928-1240

Concepts or quotes are identified at the site they appear

Commentaries
Thru The Bible J. Vernon McGee Thomas Nelson
The Bible Exposition Commentary/Prophets Warren W. Wiersbe Victor/Cook
The Bible Exposition Commentary/New Testament Vol. 2 Warren W. Wiersbe Victor/Cook
The MacArthur Bible Commentary, Unleashing God's Truth, One Verse At A Time
Copyright 2005 by John MacArthur, Printed by Thomas Nelson

ISBN: 978-1-5127-7186-2 (sc)
ISBN: 978-1-5127-7187-9 (e)

Library of Congress Control Number: 2017900539

Print information available on the last page.

WestBow Press rev. date: 02/13/2017

To Mary

With Love and a Grateful Heart

CONTENTS

Thirteen Lessons – The Letter to the Hebrews

Twenty Lessons – The Letters of James, Peter, John, Jude

FROM THE AUTHOR

Raised with a step-father predisposed to rage, my first experience with a kind and gentle man was outside the home in the person of a Boy Scout leader. An ex-marine, he exhibited strength. But <u>he was also a gentle man and that is how I remember him</u>. Certainly men who coach little league or serve as Boy Scout leaders must demonstrate strength. But it remains, these men may be the only gentle and kind man a boy experiences. Too often in our culture however, strength is synonymous with macho. Nothing can be further from the truth.

There is such a push to elevate being a macho male that gentleness and kindness, even empathy is lost. In our epidemic of gun violence and road rage, unkindness is pervasive. Gun violence from a male family member is more ominous than from an intruder. If we look at the attributes of the fruit of the Spirit, "love, joy, peace, patience, kindness, goodness, faithfulness, gentleness and self-control," macho is not among them.

The term *man up* we hear so much today is not a term that comes from the Bible. Still, we hear the term used by some Christians. *Man up* usually means to get aboard with their personal appetites. How about the term, *gentle up or kind up?* The only thing a Christian should *man up* to, is to *measure up* – to Christ Jesus.

The world to come is going to last forever. Jesus did not go to <u>prepare a place for macho males</u>, bullies if you will, only gentle kind ones like Himself. The Sermon on the Mountain attests to this fact. Many are unfamiliar with the kind of man Jesus was. Learning about Him is the beauty of Bible study. Studying the life of Jesus reveals the character of a man the wise among us would want to emulate. <u>But no one can be what he hasn't learned</u>!

Is gentleness and goodness a call for weakness? To the contrary, Scripture calls us to put on the full Armor of God. In this very dangerous world, we must accurately identify the wolves in sheep's clothing. We cannot identify the enemy via TV or radio and certainly not by our own personal appetites and preferences. <u>We can only identify the enemy by the Word of God</u>! Church is a great source for truth but we can't just simply hang our hats on sermons.

Speaking as one who has heard many wonderful sermons, I still remained biblically illiterate. Biblical literacy came by way of <u>attending a hands-on Bible study class</u>. Aided by books such as this one, engage a Bible study class or start one in your home. Welcome to Bible study! Bring a pencil.

LOOK IT UP! WRITE IT DOWN!

I spoke of hearing marvelous sermons yet remained biblically illiterate. All of us learned core subjects such as grammar, math, history and biology by means of a pencil and a workbook. I believe heavily, a workbook in combination with an overview is superior to lecture alone. There is no substitute for cementing information than to look it up and write it down! And, a workbook affords the opportunity for interactive discussion. It is amazing how much we learn from others.

Do older adults want to go back to school and prepare lessons? NO! Now you know why I prepare the workbooks we use. The pedagogy, and this is important, for a residential Bible study *must fit* to keep the group returning year after year. We briefly tried studies that provide answers in the back of the book but found they discouraged discussion and required little in the way of looking up related Scripture. Looking up Scripture is invaluable to discovering the geography of your Bible.

A pastor once told me, a study that does not require some page turning is too dumbed down to be of much value. Even though these studies are relatively brief, they require examining other parts of your Bible apart from the subject being studied.

NEVER CEASE LEARNING

"Ask and it will be given to you;
seek and you will find;
knock and the door will be opened to you."
(Matthew 7:7)

This verse is my favorite to encourage people to attend a Bible study. Like piano lessons, weekly accountability pays dividends.

Some see this verse as relating to necessities. Others errantly relate the verse to God being a vending machine dispensing material goodies. For me, it is for God to open His Word up to me. Beloved, He has done this for me and our class members. They feel blessed when making new discoveries about God and about themselves.

As you study God's Word, do so with the intent to grow your relationship with your Lord and Savior. For certain, Bible study should never be viewed as a means to earn brownie points with God.

BE A TEACHER

"Do you understand what you are reading, Phillip asked?"
How can I, he said, unless someone explains it to me?"
(Matthew 7:7)

Truly, none of us can pass on information we ourselves do not possess. A young believer often looks to an older believer for clarifications. We either give it to them or we know our way around the Bible to tell them where to look. If a skeptic asks why you believe in Jesus and you reply 'well I just do, this is no witness to the lost! To them, faith and belief are foolishness. Skeptics need reasons and we need to give it to them! Faith is fitting when around other believers. But regarding the lost, we must *be equipped* to know why we have faith. If anyone ever told you faith is blind, they are wrong. Fulfilled prophecy is a reason to believe. Eyewitness accounts of the Apostles is another. Creation is yet another. The writers of the Bible were separated by centuries, yet all point to Christ. Isn't that just simply amazing? Absolutely, faith is on solid ground! To be an effective messenger of Christ requires the principles of Colossians 3:16, 2 Timothy 4:2 and 1 Peter 3:15.

AND FINALLY

Life's path takes many turns. If God has a purpose, sometimes He will relocate you. There are numerous examples in Scripture where God relocated His servants. In my life, biblical literacy was sorely needed. Efficacy to God was a matter of geography, literally. Relocation opened the door for meeting my wife Mary in Albuquerque, New Mexico. She gifted me with a leather-bound Bible with my name etched on the cover. A feeling came over me that I had never experienced. It was as if viewing my name written in the Lamb's Book of Life! I was charged to do something with it!

But who would teach me? There was an Ethiopian in Acts 8 who needed Phillip to get him up to speed. At Mary's insistence, we attended a Tuesday night Bible study. It was a first for me. There I met a man who would indeed be my Phillip. He was a godly man named Bob Jefferson, a learned lay leader and Teaching Director of a Community Bible Study in Albuquerque. Subsequently, the knowledge I came to, God blessed me the opportunity to share with others in our community for years to come. The gift of my first Bible and attending my first Bible Study was Mary's service to the Lord. It is with love and a grateful heart I dedicate this book to her.

Give the gift of a Bible to someone.
Inscribe their name on it.
Some will be offended,
But no matter,
You may save a soul.

ACKNOWLEDGMENTS

For a Longsuffering Creator, full of Patience and generous of Grace. For Bob Jefferson, a godly man and gifted CBS Teaching Director whom God placed along my path. The men and women of Heritage Ranch and Villas in the Park communities of Fairview Texas who faithfully attended Tuesday night Bible study classes my wife and I established. And finally, my loving and supportive wife Mary, who began my personal journey to scriptural literacy by literally forcing me to attend a CBS Bible study. Always at my side, she is the spark for every class meeting. Without her set of eyes and able grammatical skills, there would be no end to my run-on-sentences. For the commentaries of gifted men and women whom God granted so much insight. And the Word itself; it is the teacher's teacher.

I mustn't forget music and all who make worship music available. Being a music person, we begin each class with music to set the tone from the toils of the day. We end each class singing "As We Go." This soft and gentle song is a beautiful way to end a Bible study. It is published by LifeWay Press.

These studies were prepared by a lay person for general enlightenment. They will not require the preparation time rigorous in depth studies demand..... John Pennington

Because of where Jesus is today, you have a hope for tomorrow

Jesus is,
God Invisible now seen by men.
Savior, Teacher, and Friend.
King of Kings and Lord of Lords.
Come, bow thy knee.

As Mary and I walked the stone paths of the Via De La Rosa in November 2013 we both remained quiet, at times tearful. We had just come from the Mount of Olives, the Garden of Gethsemane and entered Jerusalem's old city through the Joppa Gate. We had stood at the place where the night before He was crucified, Jesus prayed, anticipated, and resigned Himself to His mission and His purpose. In love, He would give Himself up for us, submitting to being nailed to a tree! By His sacrifice our sins are forgiven. Through Him, all who receive Him are forever reconciled to the Father.

With its shops and barking street vendors, the Via De La Rosa is quite different than in Jesus' day. To walk where Jesus walked is added strength to walk as Jesus taught. To love one another. Within the walls of the Church of the Holy Sepulcher one gets a surreal sense of what happened here. Events forever changing the world and the destiny of those who love the Lord above all. This is the First Commandment. If you have not studied about the Lord Jesus, do so without delay! He is your Savior, He is your Friend. Let Him also be your Teacher. He will teach you by the only means available, the Bible. If no group is available, form one. Two or three people are all you need, don't delay, bow thy knee. He is King of Kings and Lord of Lords.

"For God so loved the world that He gave His only Son. That who so ever would believe on Him shall have ever lasting life." (John 3:16)

HOW GREAT THOU ART

FOREWORD

From thirty-seven thousand miles away, Apollo 17 Astronaut Eugene Cernan snapped this remarkable picture of the earth suspended in space. The picture affirms the words of the Apostle Paul; *"For since the creation of the world, God's invisible qualities - His eternal power and divine nature have been clearly seen."* In regard to the coming Judgment and unbelieving men, Paul writes; *"being understood from what has been made, men are without excuse."* Romans 1:20

From Cernan's photo, it is inconceivable that a Creator is not behind such a fantastic physical fact. To believe the earth, its properties and the millions of life forms living on this celestial body is the result of random events requires far more faith than does believing a Creator exists. Can an atheist travel Cernan's path and still maintain there is no Creator? Assuredly, he would have to be mad to view an earth suspended in space, surrounded by millions of celestial bodies and conclude all of this a random accident! *"Where were you when I laid the foundations of the earth?"* Job 38:4

As assuredly as God exists, would He not also communicate with those who were made in His Image? *"So God created man in His own image, in the image of God He created him; male and female He created them."* Genesis 1:27 One would think that a being who could create from nothingness all that is, men would hunger to hear what He has to say. Sadly, this is not the case. Most people are too caught up with themselves to have any desire to have interest even in this Being, who has put on display His magnificence!

By your study of the Bible you have said, "I acknowledge God is real and I want to know the mind of my Glorious Creator. For if I know His mind, I will come to better know and serve Him."

One who loves the Lord is truly sanctified
One who loves the Lord prays for wisdom, strength and vision
He trust God for every need, every decision.

THE BIBLE

This book contains the mind of God, the state of man, the way of salvation, the doom of sinners, and the happiness of believers.

Its doctrines are holy, its precepts are binding, its histories are true, and its decisions are immutable.

Read it to be wise, believe in it to be safe, and practice it to be holy.

It contains light to direct you, food to support you and comfort to cheer you.

It is the traveler's map, the pilgrim's staff, the pilot's compass, the soldier's sword, and the Christian's charter.

Here paradise is restored, heaven opened, and the gates of hell disclosed.

Christ is its grand object; our good its design; and the glory of God, its end.

It should fill the memory, rule the heart, and guide the feet.

Read it slowly, frequently, and prayerfully.

It is a mine of wealth, a paradise of glory, and a river of pleasure.

It is given you in life, will be opened in the Judgment, and be remembered forever.

It involves the highest responsibility, will reward the greatest labor, and will condemn all who trifle with its sacred contents. Middletown Bible Church

Keys to Successful Study

Understand that from the story being told a principal(s) is being taught:

1. Underline key verses.
2. Circle key words.
3. Where and when the story takes place.
4. Picture yourself present!
5. Who is speaking and to whom?
6. What is the one speaking describing?
7. What or why is the person speaking?

Most mistakes for misunderstanding Scripture are due to not being aware of the context in which the speaker is referring to. It is always a good idea to examine preceding verses, even referring back to the beginning of a chapter.

USING THESE STUDIES

These studies are designed for small groups of likeminded people meeting weekly at the same time and location. The large print makes them advantageous for senior communities. The lessons are useful for individual, couple or family study and are easily understood by those with little to moderate knowledge of the Bible. If you have never attended a Bible study, these studies are for you!

Leading the studies is successful by one person or a couple. Leaders with limited preparation or knowledge should use the 'Helicopter Overview' following the discussion questions. For those living in a restricted community such as senior living or gated HOA, it is recommended a resident serve as leader. Non-resident leaders, even if seminary trained are discouraged! The most well intended non-resident in time becomes inconsistent with outside conflicts as class after class is canceled. Soon, the group dissipates or a resident must step up and lead to save the class anyway. Do occasionally invite a seminary trained guest speaker.

The studies were prepared by a lay person and can be led by an untrained believer willing to serve! Recall, not one Disciple Jesus called was qualified. Yet no one today disputes the statement of the Apostle's Creed. The Word is the real teacher! God didn't call the qualified, He qualified the called! God equips His people! These studies have been successfully tested using lay leaders for ten years. No one ever indicated anything other than, how much they had grown in their knowledge of God.

Rotating leaders is acceptable in the beginning until it is clear one person or a couple are gifted facilitators. Dependable leaders with people skills makes a class go. Ultimately, Scripture does the teaching.

The studies are drawn from the NIV Bible. In a class, read only the chapter being studied. [Also read aloud bracketed verses]. Reference verses apart from the study need not be read. Involve everyone in reading! To keep things moving, [bracketed verses] are best read by one person who has them located ahead of time. Occasionally you will find **'TIME OUT'** sections that extend beyond the chapter being studied.

These studies are not intended to make one a biblical scholar but rather, to develop a loving relationship with Jesus. God's Grace in Christ is not fully appreciated until His Word is studied. If your lack of knowledge embarrasses you, get over it and get started! One day you will leave this life. Don't let that day descend on you without fully knowing your Lord and Savior. Know more today about Jesus then you knew yesterday. As your knowledge of Him increases, so shall your love for Him Grow.

Thirteen Lessons
The Letter to the

Hebrews

Authorship Not Documented

ABOUT HEBREWS

Could a woman have penned the letter to the Hebrews? (Priscilla, Romans 16) This might explain why the lack of authorship. 2 Peter 3:15 and Romans 9:1-5 suggests Paul authored Hebrews. But could 1 Timothy 2:7 rule him out? Not necessarily, Paul loved his people as Romans 9-11 reveals. Paul did always write to a targeted church with individuals identified by name, including himself. The fact there is no geographical target suggests the letter was a call for Hebrews everywhere, to accept Christ as the promised Messiah. Irregardless, most agree, authorship is irrelevant.

The Levitical Priesthood and its sacrificial system failed to overcome the continual sin of Israel. God in His Grace, personally covered their sins and correspondingly, welcomed all who would seek refuge in Jesus. Hebrews holds a position second only to Romans validating the Christian Faith.

Hebrews is a comparative study. Key words *better than* and *more than* make the case for Christ being superior to the subject being addressed. The plurality of today's religious ideas are completely impugned by Hebrews. The concept of many ways to God is the heresy growing among some liberals. Hebrews emphatically refutes anything or anyone equal to Christ! Embracing plurality, a ritual/works centered church or a church founded by anyone other than Christ places one in great danger.

Hebrews contains a hall of fame of the Faith. Prior to Christ, Faith made these individuals righteous in God's sight. *"Abraham believed God and righteousness was credited unto him."* (Hebrews 6:2) Belief and Faith are synonymous with trusting God.

You and I have an advantage over the individuals identified in Hebrews. We have the Gospels, the Epistles and fulfilled Prophecy. With such advantages, it is amazing the unbelief with us today. The Spirit calls everyone to God's saving Grace. The problem is of the will. Hearts are hardened to hear the Spirit's call. Self-wills are just simply too obstinate to bend some knees and bow some heads.

Hebrews will enrich your life, strengthen your faith and bring you to tears of joy knowing God made the man Jesus the way of reconciliation. Assuredly, that day is coming when you will stand in the presence of Him who personally paid your debt granting you everlasting life. May our lives reflect our love for Jesus and just how thankful we are God loved us so much, that by His Grace, we are reconciled to Him.

With Hebrews comes this understanding. All must atone for sin and engage a High Priest to intercede for us. In Christ, we have the perfect Sacrifice and perfect Intercessor rolled into one. Hebrews is a must study for believers!

HEBREWS 1
The New Kid on the Block

Recent Jewish converts to Christ were always in danger of being <u>pulled back</u> into Jewish traditions to which they were certainly well schooled. Today, the danger lies in being <u>pulled aside</u> to pluralism and a myriad of cults and karmas. God's final word has come to us in the person of Jesus. (John 1:1, 14) *"I am the way, no one comes to the Father except through me."* (John 14:6) <u>Chapters one and two compare Christ to angels</u>.

Read Hebrews 1:1-14

1) After years of doing things a certain way or believing a certain way, how difficult do you find it to change your old ways of thinking and doing?

Discussion:

2) What is the key ingredient that must accompany change of mind? _____

3) When a new truth becomes evident to you, do you think it is foolish to resist?

4) In the Old Testament, God spoke to His people through dreams, angels and the prophets. Why would speaking through the Son be a better way of communication?

5) Put verse two with Revelation 22:18-19. It is arrogant for individuals to come along after Christ has spoken and claim to have received new revelations from God? Really? Arrogance is compounded when addendums to God's Word are introduced.

   a. Explain the threat of false prophets to people who are searching?

   b. Do you think the Church is too preoccupied in attacking government, gays and abortion clinics rather than issuing warnings of cults and opportunists?

6) What does Psalm 91:11-12, Exodus 3:2, 20:20-23 have in common?

7) How does the first verse identify the author of this letter to be Jewish?

8) What charge has been given to Jesus? See Psalm 2:6-9

9) By what means does God declare His glory that it is seen by men? (V.3)

10) Compare verse three with Romans 1:19-20.

11) Summarize the mission Jesus completed and where is His position today? See Mark 16:19 and Revelation 1:12-18

12) Why was Jesus superior to angels? (vv. 4-5)

13) What further statement is made to Jesus' superiority to angels? (v. 6)

14) What <u>indirect implications</u> does verse six imply regarding human responsibility?

15) Write a *summary statement* how the coming of Jesus changed the world!

Summary Statement:
What was revered by Old Testament Judaism is now turned upside down by the advent of Christ.

A <u>dialogue within the Godhead</u> is recorded in much of this chapter. We observe a similar dialogue in Psalm 110. Take a moment for someone to read [Psalm 110]. We have here a <u>parenthetical approach to identifying Christ as the fulfillment of Messianic Prophecy</u>. This Psalm was used as a Coronation Psalm when the Jews elevated one of their own to a position of Kingship. Certainly David used it. Being Jewish, a reader of Hebrews would have no problem understanding that a Jewish Messiah would one day appear and now He has.

Perhaps this example might be useful. There is one God, not three. But this one God has a three-fold function. To illustrate, you are one person but you function in multiple ways; a parent, a child, a sibling, a spouse, etc... Our central-self communicates how we function in relation a given circumstance. Though we are the same person, our signals as a parent are different than our signals as a spouse.

Sits at the right hand of the Father <u>represents both Authority and Oneness</u>. Jesus is fully God! When Deity came to earth in the person of Jesus, Deity wasn't lost in this Incarnation. Jesus simply arrived as the Second Person of the Holy Trinity. To think of Jesus as less than Deity misses the whole point God is a Triune God. Not accepting this is to be aligned with the cults. Therefore, Jesus is Lord and is to be worshiped as such!

The author of Hebrews understood he was writing to Jews schooled in Mosaic Law. Some of these folks, though grounded in Christ, were still in need of reinforcement. Perhaps others had intellectually accepted Christ but had yet to receive baptism of the Spirit. The letter has evangelistic overtones in that, it appeals to Jews who have an ear for truth. This Jesus fellow IS the Prophesied Messiah?

Imagine, after years of worship services, your pastor preaches the Cross of Christ is replaced with something better. Worse, you make a living selling wood crosses. How would you receive this new message? Would you stone the pastor or would you first research your Bible to find out if such a thing were prophesied?

Fortunately, these early Jews had a solid foundation of this New Covenant. Yet it never hurts to reinforce it! <u>Comparisons is probably the best teacher here</u>. There is probably no better comparison than to compare Jesus to something already admired, accepted and respected. The case is made. Jesus is superior and why this is so!

Application

How fortunate the creator of the universe even speaks to us, especially on a personal level. No part of Creation, including our life is out of His control! Given this truth, in time of need, go first to the Lord.

Background Enrichment

Read Leviticus 1

Notes for Hebrews 1

HEBREWS 2
"He who has an ear, let him hear"

In regard to Doctrine, the message of Romans 1-8 is also the message in this chapter. In Romans, the message was to a predominantly Gentile Congregation. Here, the message is directed to Jews. We aren't told a specific location. Perhaps, wherever Jews had settled after the Diaspora. (Scattering) Verse eleven is more than a doctrinal statement, it is a promise! It is well to memorize the passage. *"Both the One who makes men holy and those who are made holy are of the same family. Jesus is not afraid to call them brothers."* (Hebrews 2:11)

Read Hebrews 2:1-9

1) According to verse two, what was the central message the angels had delivered?

2) According to verse three, what was this new message and who had delivered it?

3) How is Christ's message superior to the message of the angels in the Old Testament?

4) The Gospels of Matthew, Mark, Luke and John are God's testimonies through four eyewitnesses. What do eyewitness accounts make obvious about Jesus? (v. 4)

Discussion:
What does it suggest about God that Christ came in the form of a man rather than an angel?

5) How do verses seven and eight elevate Christ above the angels?

6) Verse five speaks of a world to come. What is that world? See Revelation 20:6

Read Hebrews 2:10-18

7) How is your relationship with a brother different from the relationship with a neighbor who lives across the street?

8) What significant thing do you do different regarding your own children that you don't do regarding the children living down the street?

9) What is the message of Romans 8:17?

10) What is the message of John 1:3 and Colossians 1:16?

11) *"Love the Lord your God with all your heart and with all your soul and with all your mind. This is the first and greatest commandment."* (Matthew 22:37-38) The Bible is clear. Even though a person is a good person and does beneficial things, in rejecting Christ he rejects God. <u>This violates the First Commandment and he or she remains under Judgment.</u>

   a. Who will pay for the sins of one outside the family of God?

   b. Who has already paid for the sins of God's family? See John 19:30

12) From verse sixteen through eighteen, what was the mission of Jesus? What ways did He fulfill His mission?

Summary Statement:

It is wise to listen to the Son whom God has sent into the world. For in Him rests the power to overcome the devil.

The concept of Jesus' superiority to angels is continued. This perhaps seems a silly topic if you have been a lifelong follower of Christ. Herein lies the problem of successful Evangelism. <u>What you accept and take for granted is just not the same mindset of one who is lost</u>. They probably don't hold admiration for angels but you can bet they hold admiration for something that is less than Christ. A study of <u>Hebrews can help a believer be a better witness for Christ</u>! Because you understand the mind of the unbeliever. He views himself preferable to Christ.

Even though you are Christian, this chapter is a heads up not to slumber. <u>Casual Christianity is the warning here</u>. Anyone casual in their faith easily falls victim to false teachers or becomes victims of evildoers leading them into sin. The key word in this entire chapter is *more* found in the first verse! *More* or *ever increasing* are evident throughout Scripture. Both words are associated with the growth of something. Author Beth Moore concludes that in each of our lives, something is growing. <u>Whatever grows in us will get *more* of us</u>. Will it be hatred, coldness, addiction, sensuality, perversion, selfishness, fabrications, love, joy, peace, patience, kindness, goodness, faithfulness, gentleness or self-control? She further states, the antithesis of *more* of us is *less* of us. It is up to us as to those things we wish to feed and those things we wish to starve. This we call, freewill.

Certainly we cannot control what grows or starves in the world. But we can control what grows in us. *"Live a life worthy of the Lord, bearing fruit in every good work, growing in the knowledge of God."* (Colossians 1:1 pp)

Application

Pay attention and keep on paying attention! Just knowing the Gospel is only the beginning. After believing, it is all about <u>being more than a convert</u>. We must grow. Losing ground is always a possibility, backsliding if you will. Being human, we are subject to the world around us. Therefore, it is good to meet on a regular basis with like-minded people. A Bible study group meeting regularly is an excellent avenue to feed what needs to grow in us. Church is certainly good. But it is quite easy in church to drift into becoming simply a spectator. This writer should know. For I was nothing more than a pew sitter for forty-five years. A Bible study group more than church attendance changed that!

Background Enrichment

Read Leviticus 6:8-13

Notes for Hebrews 2

HEBREWS 3
The House Builder

Has anyone ever seen a housing development with the grounds-keeper's name inscribed on the marque instead of the builder?

The house builder is greater than the servants in the house or he who mows the grass. It is the builder to whom recognition belongs. Christ, being the builder of the Church, is greater than anyone who serves in the Church. It is in the builder to whom we trust for our shelter. This lesson escaped those who were in the desert for forty years. *"So we see that they were not able to enter, because of their unbelief."* (v. 19) Just as unbelief kept the wandering Israelites from entering the Promised Land, so shall unbelief and indifference shut the doors of Heaven.

Read Hebrews 3:1-6

1) Explain what God's Elect share together? See also 1 Peter 1:1-2

2) Jesus is identified both as an Apostle and High Priest. Explain the two functions.

3) What similarities exists between Jesus and Moses?

4) Upon what criteria does the author elevate Christ above Moses?

5) Identify the house that Jesus built. See Matthew 16:18

6) What is the message of Matthew 7:24-27?

Read Hebrews 3:7-19

7) Upon what precedent does the author issue the warning given in verses seven through eleven? See Psalm 78:40-42; 56-59

Discussion:

Do you ever think it possible that you, like the Israelites, could fall away from God? What are some safeguards against falling away?

8)	What is the greatest threat to not remaining faithful? (v. 13)

9)	Write down and memorize Proverb 4:23.

10)	What does verse sixteen and Romans 9:7a suggest can happen even to some who attend church regularly?

11)	More than anything else, what one thing will bar some from God's rest? (v. 12)

12)	Was there ever a time you had something wonderful planned for a friend or a loved one, but because of their betrayal, disgusting behavior or attitude, you withheld your plan for them? Explain.

Discussion:

If God is love and full of forgiveness, why would He deny the best for all people?

13)	What is the unforgiveable sin in the Bible? See Matthew 12:31-32

Summary Statement:

Just as Moses was selected to minister over the house of Israel, (v. 2) Jesus was God's choice to minister over the house which He would personally build, the Church. Whereas Moses was but a servant, the Son of God was the House Builder. It is to the builder we attach recognition to.

Hardening one's heart to Christ is not just a Jewish problem, it is a universal problem. A hard heart is step one to shutting the door on God's indwelling Spirit. For the individual unable to discern the Spirit's call, that person remains lost. Jesus is rejected and they live a life separated from God. That in itself is counter to the First Commandment.

Abraham, followed by Moses, are the two most admired individuals by the Jewish people. After comparing Christ to angels and prophets, Christ is now compared to Moses. The writer makes it clear, though a servant in a house is valuable, it is the builder who is the more valuable. *House* is used six times in the first six verses. It is a key word to understanding the chapter. <u>Two houses are addressed here</u>. Both are a group of people, not physical buildings. One, the house of Israel was ministered over by Moses and Aaron and the second, the body of Christ, the Church. The author wishes to emphasize to his Jewish readers which house they are now a part. He also reminds them of those of the House of Israel who did not enter into God's Promise. Only in the house the Son has built, is a man assured of entering into God's Promise.

Falling away is not a good idea.

After having been put in the care of the innkeeper with money to sustain his needs, can you imagine the victim in the <u>Parable of the Good Samaritan</u> leaving the security freely provided him and returning back out to the road where he was ambushed? <u>Sadly, that is what many do today</u>. The Good Samaritan has come and rescued us from ambush. He has given us shelter and provided for our needs until He returns. But some hardheads prefer to go back out onto that same road and continue trying to make it on their own. Falling away is perhaps an indicator one wasn't sealed in the first place.

Excerpts from Psalm 95 is a reminder that in Christ, God looks after us as He did His people coming out Egyptian bondage. <u>Today's bondage is unbelief</u>. The same fate awaits unbelievers today that befell unbelievers of the Exodus. Unbelief forfeits one's right-of-passage into God's Promised Land. The Author of Hebrews is aware, as in the desert wanderings, trials are a given. When trials do come, doubt and unbelief are not far behind. He exhorts readers to *"Fix your thoughts on Jesus."* (v. 1)

Application

"Fix your thoughts on Jesus." (v. 1)

"In my Father's house are many mansions; if it were not so I would have told you. I go to prepare a place for you. And if I go and prepare a place for you, I will come again and receive you to myself; that where I am, there you may be also." **John 14:1-3 NKJV**

Background Enrichment

Read Leviticus 21

Notes for Hebrews 3

HEBREWS 4
Approach the Throne of Mercy with Confidence

For the Jews, turning away from God's provision for them wasn't just an anomaly of the Exodus. It was ever present in their history. This Epistle addresses man's tendency to repeat history. <u>Therein is why Hebrews is relevant for the Church</u>. Many, especially our youth, have heard the Gospel in church. They listened for a while, then eventually many turned away without <u>trusting Jesus as Lord</u> of their life. Unlike the Jews who looked back at Mosaic Law, today's lost look to pluralism, various karmas, cults or simply dismiss it all.

Read Hebrews 4:1-11

1) When did you first become aware of the Gospel of Jesus Christ?

2) Did you immediately give an ear to the Gospel or did you dismiss it for a while?

3) Assuming you are saved, has there ever been a time you wavered in your faith?

Discussion:

From Bible study to character development, what things do you think a believer must hold to, to insure the work first begun in them at conversion continues?

4) What is God's reaction to those who refuse to enter His rest/provision? (v. 3)

5) How might the Sabbath day (v. 9-10), Genesis 2:1-2 and 2 Corinthians 17-19 all be inter-related?

Read Hebrews 4:12-16

6) Analyze Psalm 95.

vv. 1-2

vv. 3-5

vv. 6-7a

vv. 7b-11

7) What is the nature of God's rest? (v. 11) See Matthew 11:28-30

8) God being Spirit is not seen by mortal man. So that He might relate to our flesh, what does verse fourteen through eighteen describe God as doing?

Self-Evaluation:

How do you rank yourself as being one who fully trusts God <u>in all areas</u> of your life?

Complete Trust   Partial Trust   Almost Never   Trust Self More

Explain:

9) What might verse thirteen suggest about hidden sin or using God as a vending machine?

Summary Statement:

God rested after six days of forming Creation. Now we rest in knowing His work in the Son finished in three days formed us as a new Creation. Sadly for some, the hearing of this Gospel is of no value to them. Because they live as if they were still in the time before ever hearing the Gospel.

You are charged with a capital crime for which the punishment is death. Worse, you are guilty! You need a defense attorney. Being guilty, there is a need for an advocate of the highest order. Now you discover <u>you lack the assets to assist in your defense</u>.

This chapter is one of the more theologically complex in the Bible. Space doesn't permit the depths the chapter richly deserves. If you have an Amplified Bible handy, you might want to use it. <u>*Rest* appears eleven times</u> in the first eleven verses with a twelfth implied. From resting on the Sabbath, to being in God's rest 24/7, to eternal rest, *rest* can be symbolic of multiple circumstances. Let us simply refer to *rest* here as <u>God's planned protection pro bono</u>.

Certainly the Word of God is a place to go for strength and encouragement! But the Bible also carries warnings. The Parables of Jesus contain numerous warnings. The author of Hebrews uses historical facts to make his case to not drift back into a time when <u>unbelief condemned an entire generation</u>. This generation believed when they started out from Egypt. They believed at the Red Sea. <u>But along the way of testing</u>, and this is important, they turned from belief to unbelief.

When we trust God in some circumstances but not others, we too are in danger of falling into the situation described in this chapter. Cafeteria trusting is not a part of Christian Theology. Not trusting God usually ends in one of two ways, running ahead of Him, disobedience, or both.

Let us not confuse seeking God's rest with doing good works such as more Bible reading, better church attendance, singing in the choir, overcoming selfishness, less gossiping etc. <u>God's rest is not about us</u>! These noble acts are simply the results of being controlled by the Holy Spirit. Seeking God's rest can be boiled down to one word, *trust.* <u>Trusting what? John 3:16 is the place to start</u>. God freely sacrificing His Son as payment for our sins.

The Author of Hebrews describes God's Word as a double edged sword powerful enough to open the inner most thoughts of every individual. <u>Nothing is out of sight of God</u>. We need not get uptight over this. For Jesus understands our weakness. He Himself advocates for us. If you have been diligent in reading the recommended enrichment readings regarding the Law, Matthew 11:28-30 gives you a sigh of relief. You can with confidence, boldly approach the Throne of Grace.

If the New Covenant in Jesus is simple, why does Israel reject Him as the Messiah? They simply don't believe. In the West, the unacceptance of Jesus is in part, unbelief. But often the reason is pride. Pride prevents many knees from bowing to anyone. One day that is going to change. Isaiah 45:18-24 declares *"every knee will bow."* Seven years following the Rapture will be the day. The Second Coming will also be the fulfilment of God's final Old Testament Covenant with Israel. The Davidic Covenant, where from Jerusalem, the Messiah will reign as David's rightful descendent over Israel and all the earth.

Application

All people stand condemned! Ecclesiastes 7:20, Romans 3:10-20. At the Judgment, every sin will be paid for. Whether a person believes this is irrelevant. Unbelievers will not find rest for they will advocate for themselves. Those in Christ have promise of God's rest. His power advocates for them. On whom do you rest?

Background Enrichment

Read Leviticus 16:1-6; 29-34

Notes for Hebrews 4

HEBREWS 5
A Problem Identified

All of us like to think Christians always come to sound conclusions but often they don't. Those who believe Salvation can be gained and then lost again rest much of this belief on this chapter. But doesn't such thinking challenge the surety God knows what he is doing when He seals a person? (Revelation 7:3-4) <u>Falling from Grace should not be confused with falling into sin.</u>

When God's people failed, they were in need of an intercessor to be reconciled to God.

The Priesthood established in the manner of Aaron was itself flawed because the priests themselves were earthly. Having passed through the heavens, Christ was of the rank of Melchizedek. All His qualifications exceeded those of Aaron's line. A case can be made for Melchizedek and Christ being one and the same.

Read Hebrews 5:1-14

1) How did one become a high priest? (v. 1) <u>See notes at end of lesson for details.</u>

2) Describe the duties of a high priest and the demeanor of his character in ministering to others.

3) What is a high priest obligated to do concerning his own human failings? See Leviticus 16:2-6, 11

4) How did it come about that Christ was appointed a high priest? (v. 5)

5) a. How long will Christ remain as the high priest? (v. 6) (Psalm 110:4)

   b. What duties other than high priest are given to Christ? See Psalm 110

Discussion:
Certainly Jesus was stressed a great deal during his ministry. What one thing caused Him the most anguish?

6) What made Jesus different from all other high priest who preceded Him? See Hebrews 4:14

7) Verse eleven through fourteen is highly critical of some? What problems might be present here and what were the dangers? See Revelation 3:15-16

Time Out: Polar opposite problems sometimes exist in Christian people. Causal Christians are believers whose life style is not all that distinguishable from non- Christian. Worse are the fundamentalist bullies who use Scripture to justify violence against family or anyone they view as ungodly. They are prone to law breaking, even murder in the name of God. Finally, perversion of the law of love leads some misguided souls in support of homosexual marriage. Verse thirteen states that believers with <u>warped views of the Gospel haven't even cut their teeth yet</u>!

8) Write your definition of

   a. a mature Christian.

   b. an Immature Christian.

9) a. From your description of mature and immature, into which category best describes your Christian maturity?

   b. If you or anyone falls into the category of an immature Christian, what steps must be taken to grow in the Faith? See Romans 12:1, Galatians 5:18-26

10) Define righteous living that is Divine. (vv. 9, 14)

11) What two things must a piano student do to improve and fine tune their pianistic skills?

Summary Statement:
Good News: Having passed through the heavens, Christ is a High Priest of the highest order. The bad news; some are too immature to even engage in an intelligent conversation concerning the Faith! This is contrary to the mission of the believer. <u>For all believers are to be teachers</u>. See Colossians 3:16

The theme continues. Christ is superior! A High Priest without sin, Jesus was the perfect appointee of God. Being sinless, He never needed to atone for His own sin as had all priests before Him. The apparent tendency of Jewish converts to drift as had their ancestors, placed them in the same peril of failure. Canaan lay ahead for the people of the Exodus. But they failed to enter the rest God had prepared for them. The Millennial Kingdom lies ahead for Jewish converts. Will they enter God's rest?

Transfer the problem defined here, to today's church congregation and it boils down to this. Many have an intellectual knowledge of Jesus but lack the personal relationship to seal the deal. Like the Israelites in the desert, they fail to tie the knot of trust, so to speak, between knowledge of, and total faith in, God's Sovereignty. These are those who believe the conspiracies invented by men intent on dispensing fear. Fear is not a fruit of the Spirit and it is contrary to biblical teachings!

Still others appear godly, but much is hidden from view. Such groups share this problem, *"They have a form of godliness but deny its power."* (2 Timothy 3:5) Immature Christians hold to the view that man, not God, is in control. Some are even so naive as to believe we can vote our way out of God's ultimate plan for the ages. These are not Christians of Faith, they are Christians of circumstances. Talking to them about Sovereignty one quickly sees the thick glaze of media propaganda in their eyes.

In Christ, (not the ballot box) we have all we could ever want. When the world goes to pot, we aren't going with it. What is there to fear? If you are not familiar with 1 Thessalonians 4:13-18, get familiar! It is one of the most *restful* sections in all Scripture. Revelation 19-20 to the conclusion is also quite *restful*.

In the meantime, love the work God has given you to *rest* in in this life. Oswald Chambers has a book, "My Utmost for His Highest" that is a must read for today's believer. When Christ returns, the faithful will not have lived in fear or will they have anything to hide. Those who do have hidden things will be exposed by the double edged sword of the Word of God.

Application

MATTURITY		IMMATTURITY
Able to instruct others	rather than	always the learner
Develops depth of understanding	rather than	never advances beyond the basics
Accurate self-evaluation	rather than	blames others for failings
Seeks unity	rather than	ostracize others, motive to divide
Desire spiritual filling	rather than	seeking to be entertained
Discerns truth from spin	rather than	has itching ears
Active faith	rather than	cafeteria trust of God
Embraces the Sovereignty of God	rather than	marches to fear's drumbeat

Modified from Life Application Study Bible
Tyndale House Publisher, Inc. Wheaton, Illinois and Zondervan Publishing House Grand Rapids, Michigan

Background Enrichment

Read Leviticus 8:6-29

Notes for Hebrews 5

High Priest Comparisons:

Leviticus 8:1-6	Corinthians 6:11
Washed in water	Washed in blood
Leviticus 8:7-9	Isaiah 61:10
Garments	Dressed in His righteousness
Leviticus 8:10-12	1 Peter 1:18
Blood sacrifice	Sacrifice/Redeemed
Leviticus 8:13-29	1 John 2:20, 27
Anointed by oil	Anointed by the Spirit

HEBREWS 6
Maturity Erases Doubt

When a Bible chapter begins with the word therefore, as this one, it is advisable to go back and examine the end of the previous chapter. The writer of Hebrews is adamant, if you have chosen to follow the Lord Jesus, then learn the program! The analogy of public education is used to illustrate Christian maturity. When a child enrolls in the first grade, he doesn't expect to still be sitting in the first grade twelve years later!

Read Hebrews 6:1-6

1) Was there ever a time you doubted your high school diploma was insufficient to put you in a position to enter college or the workplace?

2) With the aid of a dictionary, define vacillate. Are doubt and vacillation related?

3) In what way did Satan use doubt to deceive Eve? See Genesis 3:1

4) What contributes to a newborn baby growing stronger, the passing of time or the nourishment received from food that is eaten?

5) Who is better equipped to give care and instruction to a child, another child or an adult?

6) Verse one speaks of works that lead to death. The context here is not about sinful works. The works here are about good works. How can it be that good works would lead to death?

7) If good works cannot earn eternal life, what must we do to be saved? See John 10:9 and Acts 16:30-31

Read Hebrews 6:7-12

8) Compare verses seven and eight with Matthew 13:1-9

9) God knows your good works. (Revelation 2:2) Still, good works are not what saves us. So what is the purpose of good works? See Matthew 5:16

10) We all like to see evidence that something is so! What does Matthew 5:16 and 2 Timothy 3:17 say about evidence that one is who he believes himself to be?

Read Hebrews 6:13-20

11) What is an oath?

12) a. What oath did God make to Abraham that He swore by His name to fulfill?

   See Genesis 22:16-18

   b. What is the message of Revelation 3:5?

Discussion:

What evidence can we have that a person who takes an oath to do something kept his word?

13) Under the Law, only the high priest was allowed behind the curtain in the Temple. What changed and what brought about this change? See Matthew 27:50-52

Summary Statement:

"God wanting to make the unchanging nature of his purpose very clear to the heirs of <u>what was promised</u>, <u>He confirmed</u> it with an oath. God did this so that, by two unchangeable things in which it is impossible for God to lie," (vv. 17-18) God is neither fickle or is He wishy-washy. Once saved, sealed forever! See Ephesians 4:30, John 6:39

How did you answer the first question of this lesson? Was there ever a time you doubted your high School diploma was sufficient to place you in a position to enter college or the workplace? Beloved, Christ is more sufficient than a high school diploma! (Turn in this lesson book and examine the addendum to 1 Peter 1 about position change)

This chapter is misunderstood by those who say Salvation can be lost. They believe you can anger God to the point He unseals you. <u>Beloved, this is not so!</u> Certainly we grieve the Spirit when we sin. But to doubt your Salvation, that is the devil doing a number on you just as he planted the seed of doubt in Eve. *Did God say?* (Genesis 3:1)

People who say Salvation can be lost are ignorant teachers who have been deceived by the devil. Our God does not retract His promises. <u>Remember the thief on the cross</u>! He had no time for baptism or good works to earn Salvation. There was not a doubt in his mind about Jesus' ability to save him! <u>He was saved by faith alone</u>. (Luke 23:42-43)

Veterans who saw action in WWII will tell you of foxhole conversions. Imminent death is a great motivator. Everyone will ultimately come face to face with death. Neither water baptism nor good works plays a role in battlefield Salvation. Does this mean baptism and works are not necessary? Absolutely not! Both give glory to God as <u>both are witnesses before men</u>. But neither are witnesses before God. <u>Christ alone is our witness before God</u>! Let us never doubt, Faith alone saves!

"I will never leave you or forsake you" (Joshua 1:5) When we vacillate or doubt our Salvation, assuredly we grieve the Spirit. But beloved, remembrance of Him is evidence and assurance He remembers you! To allow doubt to creep into one's faith is tantamount to going back to the first grade. In essence, crucifying Christ all over again! Let us graduate then, forward into a deeper understanding of the Word. Securing for our self, a more mature relationship with the Savior.

There are two stages in Christianity, faith and being. Being demands maturing. Peter was aware that some new converts were still stuck on the issue of faith and works and making little progress towards <u>becoming the kind of person that gives glory and honor to God</u>. There is a school of thought today that suggests such a person might not have been saved in the first place. Matthew 7:15-23.

Application

<u>This chapter is a call to mature, not doubt!</u>

Pray this prayer. Father, I thank you for rescuing me from my transgressions and receiving me into your family. Help me to never doubt your Word or worry about being removed from your family. My assurance Lord is not in the doubt others plant. My assurance is in the One whom I know and trust. Amen

"For I am convinced that neither death nor life,
neither angels nor demons, neither the present nor the future, nor any
powers, neither height nor depth, nor anything else in all creation,
will be able to separate us from the love of God
that is in Christ Jesus our Lord."

Romans 8:38-39

Background Enrichment

Read Mark 7:1-13

Notes for Hebrews 6

HEBREWS 7
The Mysterious Priest

Melchizedek is an unfamiliar name to the average church goer. So why might his name be significant in the New Testament? Because of what Melchizedek and Christ have in common.

The author here is not communicating with Gentiles. He is addressing Jewish Christians knowledgeable of historic Israel in regard to figures identified with Abraham. Melchizedek, besides being a contemporary of Abraham, was the high water mark of the Jewish Priesthood. Christ's comparison to Melchizedek was of major significance.

Read Hebrews 7:1-10

1) Considering ancient times was a time of pagan worship, what unique thing did Melchizedek do that is pleasantly surprising? See Genesis 14:19-20

2) What was Abraham's response to being blessed by Melchizedek? (v. 1)

3) Salem was an ancient city many suggest was an early name for Jerusalem. How might Psalm 76:1-2 suggest Salem and Jerusalem are one and the same?

Discussion:

Unlike most figures given a position of importance in Scripture, Melchizedek is without genealogy in regard to parents or children. Also, priests served God until their death when another priest would replace them. But the author states in verse three, Melchizedek's priesthood was without a beginning or end. What might this suggest about Melchizedek? See Psalm 110:1, 4

Read Hebrews 7:11-22

4) Verse eleven identifies the Tribe of Levi as the source of supply for the priesthood associated with Mosaic Law. What is pointedly different about Christ's priesthood?

5) What is the case the writer of Hebrews makes in verses eighteen, nineteen, twenty-six and twenty-seven that Christ was better than the Law to draw men closer to God?

6) From verses eighteen and nineteen, what one thing did both the Old and New Covenants require? (**Note:** This is a one word answer)

7) a. With God, what is the significance of blood?

   b. Under the New Covenant, what cleanses you and me clean that we may boldly approach the Throne of God? See Hebrews 4:16, Revelation 7:14

Read Hebrews 7:23-28

8) Relate verse twenty-four to 1 John 2:1 and explain the service Jesus provides for you and me at the Throne of Heaven.

9) How does verse twenty-five explain Christ's Priesthood being superior to the priesthood of men?

10) What two things are all men and women destined for one day? (v. 27)

Discussion:

Because of what Jesus *finished*, works are no longer needed by you and me to be acceptable in the eyes of God. What do you say to a believer who lives as if Jesus has given believers a free pass to sin?

11) What does Romans 12:1-2 instruct believers to do?

Summary Statement:

Peace with God is attained only on the basis of righteousness. Mosaic Law made no man righteous because it depended upon continuous animal sacrifice administrated by a succession of less than perfect men. Christ was sacrificed once to take away the sins of many. Correspondingly, His Priesthood is equal to His sacrifice. There is no further need for a continuation of an ongoing succession of priests.

Jewish people and Christians today knowledgeable of Old Testament Scripture are aware that the priesthood was supplied from the Tribe of Levi. This was so from the time of the Exodus. Aaron was the first of a century's long line of priests appointed by God to serve Him and His people in the Tabernacle. All were fallible men whom themselves required atonement for sin before they could act on behalf of others. The writer of Hebrews makes his case, from the advent of Christ, there is no longer any need for the Levitical Priesthood line to continue. Purity had replaced impurity. Three points are made for Christ in the opening verses.

First, Melchizedek was both a priest and a king. This was in direct violation of Mosaic Law. Under Levitical law, no man could act in both capacities. Second, the name Melchizedek means both *king of righteousness* and *king of peace.* The area of Melchizedek's kingship was Salem or shalom which in the Hebrew means peace. Thirdly, Melchizedek received a *tenth* of Abraham's war profits. Meaning the <u>greater receives an offering from the lessor.</u> This set the stage for Christ to replace the Levitical Priesthood centuries before its inception.

Question: What did God foreknow?

We can't categorically conclude that Melchizedek and Christ were one and the same person. Being compared to the Son of God, having no beginning or end, we can certainly surmise Melchizedek is at minimum, identified as a prefiguration of Christ.

For the Jew, it was not acceptable for a high priest to be from any tribe except the Tribe of Levi. Jesus, having descended from the Tribe of Judah, is traced back to Jesse, father of David. David served as a king. As stated earlier, no Tribe could supply both kingship and the priesthood. <u>Jesus' break in lineage would be a radical break for the Jew</u> of the First Century. It is no wonder, much of the early persecution of Christians came at the hands of the Jews.

It is safe to say many, perhaps even believers, are unaware all need an advocate before God! The greatness of God is such that no man is worthy to appear at the Throne of Purity. After the fall, God might have shut the lot of us out of His presence. In Mercy and love, God presented Himself in the Person of Jesus to be both Sacrifice and High Priest for all who would accept Jesus! *"For God so loved the world that He gave His only begotten Son, that whomever would receive Him would have eternal life."* (John 3:16)

Application

Maintain faith in the One who is your advocate before God and who ultimately will save you from the coming Judgment.

Background Enrichment

Read Numbers 8:15-26

Notes for Hebrews 7

HEBREWS 8
The True Tabernacle

All church buildings and alters on earth are but loose replicas of the real thing. The True Tabernacle is found only in Heaven. (Revelation 4) John was privileged to witness the True Tabernacle which he describes as well as language allows. Decidedly, this chapter makes the case that Jesus' position is <u>one with God</u>. (v. 1) In short, Jesus is God! God Himself became a man through the womb of a woman in order to establish His humanity. This truth is the most twisted by false teachers and the apostate church.

Read Hebrews 8:1-8

1) Briefly, as if reporting for a newspaper, describe Heavens Throne. And if you can, what does each image represent? See Revelation 4

2) What other things of God originate from the Heavenly Tabernacle? See Revelation 15:5-8

3) What are the two things every priest is called to do? (v. 3)

4) How was Moses instructed to build the earthly Tabernacle? (v. 5)

5) In what ways does the church you attend match verse five?

6) In your words, why is the New Covenant superior to the Old Covenant Law?

7) God's Law given to Moses was not flawed, for nothing given of God is flawed. So what was the problem with the Old Covenant? (v. 8) See Hebrews 8:9-13

8) Verse seven and eight explain that the problem with the Old Covenant was not the Covenant but the people. What was the problem with people? (v. 9)

9) Instead of writings on scrolls and tablets, where will God write the New Covenant?
See Hebrews 10:16, Jeramiah 31:31-34

10) What does verses eleven, twelve and thirteen outline that has common ground with Revelation 14:6-7 and Ecclesiastes 12:13-14?

Time out: *"It is finished."* (John 19:30) Some religious sects errantly teach legalism. They leave the impression that their followers need to assist Jesus in saving them. If that were so, then Grace is watered down. The saving of us glorifies God! To God be the glory! If our help is needed, then could we not brag of our good works? Beloved, God doesn't need our help to save us! The blood of Jesus is sufficient. Legalism has no place in the New Covenant.

11) How will legalism be lethal for those who depended on it come Judgment day?

12) What does it mean to you today, knowing that Jesus not only paid for your sins, He is your advocate for your failings yesterday, today and future? (v. 12)

Summary Statement:
Considering the fallibility of the works of the human species, no one will elevate to a purity that grants them the right of passage into God's Perfect Kingdom. But we need not worry, our God of Grace and Mercy has taken it upon Himself to make what is impure, pure. He has done this in the Person of Jesus Christ.

The question could be asked, if only Christ can save, what is the purpose of the Law? The purpose of the Law was to identify sin! If we know what sin is and what the wages of sin are going to be, then we will have a better appreciation of our Merciful God and what He did for us in the Person of Christ Jesus.

Many today falsely believe that being a good person, being ethical, helping others, giving to charitable organizations makes them right with God. Others believe serving in their church or membership in a particular religious sect puts them in good standing with God! Nonsense! Such conclusions are the devil's deception. Just as the serpent deceived Eve into doubting Gods instructions, the devil deceives people to believe they don't need Christ. Or that Christ needs our help. *"Your enemy the devil prowls around like a roaring lion, seeking whom he can devour."* (1 Peter 5:8) Beloved, no one can good their way to heaven. No religious sect, no amount of goodness displaces the work at the Cross. For pure was sacrificed for impure. Still others are deceived to believe heaven and hell don't exist. How tragic! Being they weren't around at Creation, how they know this is anybody's guess. The day they cross behind the veil it will be too late! Beloved, the Word of God is clear. *"Salvation is found in no one else, for there is no other name under heaven given to men by which we must be saved."* (Acts 4:12) Living apart from Christ Jesus is living apart from God.

This chapter is a continuation of Chapter 7. In that chapter, Christ was discussed in relation to an earthly priesthood, specifically Melchizedek. Chapter 8 identifies Christ with the true Tabernacle of Heaven. He is also identified as representing a better Covenant. Of note, and this is important, Christ is seated! When a priest takes a seat, it means *his work is finished.* In the Old Testament, there were no chairs in the Tabernacle because the work of the priest is never finished! But now in Jesus, atonement has been made. Sin has been satisfied and man's relationship, broken in the Garden of Eden, is restored. *"It is finished!"* (John 19:30) An acceptable Sacrifice has been made and never again in need of repeating. Sin has been satisfied. Humankind is reconciled with God.

Jesus' seat in Heaven is exaltation of the highest order. He is there now, advocating for all who come to the Father by and through Him. The devil accuses you and me day and night but Jesus intercedes on our behalf. (Revelation 12:10) He laid down his life on our behalf.

Beloved, if anyone does not have Christ, he is in a state of war with the Father. Having rejected God's Grace in Jesus, that person is without an ally. He will have to fend for himself on Judgment day!

Application

Scripture is clear, Israel, the smallest and weakest of nations is the apple of God's eye. Out of Her our Merciful God grew His Church so that all the world might be saved. (John 3:16) Love Israel and Her People.

Background Enrichment

Read Exodus 25:8-22

Notes for Hebrews 8

HEBREWS 9
Worship and Sacrifice, Then and Now

By now, you have a picture of Old Testament sacrifices, manner of worship and rigid specifications at the worship site. What freedom we have today! Not the least of which is not to have to engage in what most certainly was one grisly scene. As we thank our Lord, let us consider the whole of what He has done for us that has lightened our burden. Memorize Matthew 11:30

Read Hebrews 9:1-10

1) What were the names of the two locations in the Old Covenant Tabernacle?

2) What separated the Holy Place from the Holy of Holies?

3) What three items appeared in the Holy Place?

4) Describe the contents of the Holy of Holies.

5) The information given us in Matthew 27:50-52 indicates something significant had just occurred. What is it?

6) Which room did the daily work of the priests take place? _____

7) Which room was limited to the high priest alone? _____

8) What was the limitation of the high priest in regard to entering the Holy of Holies?

9) What was it that the sacrifices being made did not do? (v. 9)

Read Hebrews 9:11-15

10) What is self-righteous works?

Discussion:

Why is the person in Christ going to be infinitely cleaner at the Judgment than the individual who perhaps was even a better person but who regrettably had rejected Christ? If you are unsure, see Revelation 7:14

11) Verse fourteen speaks of *works that lead to death*. Is the author speaking of immoral acts only or might he be speaking of moral acts?

Note: To answer this question accurately, you must know what the term *"dead works"* mean. See Proverbs 14:12 and 16:25

Discussion:

Might there be a conflict with *works* in verse fourteen with James 2:14-20?

Time Out: Just as not everyone goes to church, not all Jews participated in the animal sacrificial system. *"Those who are called"* (v. 15) has to do with the participants in animal sacrifices, who by faith can be associated with Abraham. Do not try to use verse fifteen to justify reason to support an election argument concerning Gentiles prevalent in the Church today. We are speaking here of Jews in Old Testament times that those who believed God <u>by faith were saved on credit</u>. (John 8:56, Romans 4:20-22) Christ saved all, past, present and future.

Read Hebrews 9:16-28

12) What life source did Jesus spill to save us? _____

Discussion:

Beloved, you are saved because you were washed by the blood of the Lamb! (Revelation 7:14) If you have been taught and believe that water baptism saves you, then you must believe the blood of the Lamb wasn't enough! The Thief on the cross refutes such a conclusion. It would say foxhole conversions and death-bed conversions are invalid. Certainly water Baptism is not to be rejected when the life of the believer continues? Why is this?

13) What does verse twenty-seven promise for every person living?

Summary Statement:

In Christ, one's good works serve to glorify God. Apart from Christ, *all* good works are simply the world's system of self-righteousness. Jesus will appear a second time, not to again bear sin, but to glorify those who are waiting for Him! Maranatha!

Unless you have been keeping up with your Levitical Readings it is impossible to fully appreciate the words of Jesus when He said, *"My yoke is easy, my burden is light."* What is expected of the Church no longer requires the cutting up of animals. This unpleasantness has been forever satisfied with the blood of the Lamb of God. Being free from Mosaic Law however does not set aside responsibility. Through the ministry of Jesus and the New Testament Epistles, a different set of responsibilities are given to the Church. Giving up ourselves to Christ replaces giving up a prized bull. Because He gave Himself up for us, we are called to love Him and respond in kind by giving ourselves to Him. [Read Romans 12:1-2]

Draw your attention to verse fourteen. This verse relates to not being deceived that good works or being moral plays a role in Salvation. *"Cleanse our consciences from acts that lead to death."* Good works and morality are the Fruit of Salvation. Let us be clear, verse fourteen has nothing to do with immoral actions. Certainly the wages of sin lead to death. But here the author is speaking of moral acts the well-meaning person places his faith in, believing his good deeds, not Christ, will save him from Judgment. We must all be aware that since the fall of man, all men are dead in sin. Therefore, dead men's works are equally as dead as they are. Only Christ makes one's works alive and pleasing to God.

> *"All of us have become like one who is unclean,*
> *and all our righteous acts are like filthy rags."*
>
> **Isaiah 64:6**

Let us repeat, it is not a case of too much wrong with the Old Covenant, it is a case of too much wrong with us.

Application

There is in Heaven today, the real Tabernacle. A permanent one! It is presided over by a Great High Priest. He ministers in every corner of the globe. He can be called upon from any location. He hears your prayers. Give your burdens over to Him. You do not have to first wash your hands, prepare a bowl of water, light candles or adjust furniture. Simply look up and reassign your heart and mind to Him. He is waiting.

Apart from Christ, there is no glory in deeds. For even good deeds lead to death. Purge your conscience from thoughts that your works are the way to eternal life. Glory in the Christ!

Background Enrichment

Read Exodus 33:7-11

Notes for Hebrews 9

HEBREWS 10
The First is replaced by the Second

Verse eight reveals a practice Israelites were instructed to follow regarding marriage and servitude. It has to do with whether a master gave a servant a wife or if the servant provided himself a wife. Hopefully we can understand in simple terms, the case here is, Jesus was provided as a sin offering as opposed to the sinner providing his own sin offering. See Exodus 21:1-6

Part A - Read Hebrews 10:1-24 – Confidence contributes to perseverance.

1) What was the purpose of repetitive animal sacrifice? (v. 3)

2) In what ways might lingering guilt affect a person's life and their relationships?

3) a. Have you ever experienced lingering guilt?

   b. What did you do about it?

4) Name the principle reason the sacrificial system was done over and over?

5) What is the bottom line message of verses five, six and seven? See Psalm 40:6-8

6) Name the many ways Christ was qualified to be the Perfect Sacrifice for sin?

7) What three things are said of Jesus in verses nineteen, twenty and twenty-one?

8) What is the significance of Jesus' body being called a curtain? See Hebrews 6:19

9) What three commands does the author issue in verses twenty-two, twenty-three and twenty-four?

Part B - Read Hebrews 10:25-39 – Let us go forth and not draw back.

Time Out: Prior to Christ, the sacrificial system was done in obedience to God's commands. But God has given a better command replacing the first. But many in the early church continued practicing the old sacrificial system. These religious acts were of no value. Such people exist today. They observe church devised rituals believing this is part of their Salvation. <u>Rituals compromise thankfulness and inhibits developing a loving relationship with our Lord</u>. Much of this is an attempt to present an image of piety. *"Not everyone who says to me, Lord, Lord, will enter the kingdom of heaven."* (Matthew 7:21)

Discussion:

2 Peter 1:10 teaches that if one is indeed saved, there will be evidence. What kind of evidence do you look in determining if a person you just met is a Christian?

10) Romans 8:29-30 and similar Scriptures assure us, once a person has been saved from Satan's grasp, the Good Shepherd does not let him slip away. That said, what might you believe about a person who says they are saved but they never gather with other believers?

11) What are the benefits of gathering on a regular basis with other believers?

Discussion:

What is obvious when a person says their religion is too private to discuss?

12) Has God ever taken you to the woodshed? (v. 31) _____

13) What is the message of 1 Peter 4:17-18?

14) What is the final encouragement the author ends the chapter with?

Summary Statement:

<u>Nothing can be written on an unsteady heart</u>! Before God writes His Commands on the heart and mind, He first tests one's perseverance. For the one who is weak, perseverance escapes him, because he is *"tossed back and forth by the waves, and blown here and there by every wind of teaching."* (Ephesians 4:14)

The carpet at your front door trips people. For months you have told your children to enter the house through the back door after school. But now you purchase a new rug and put it in place at the front door. You move the old rug to the back door. You inform your kids it is OK to enter the front door because there is a new rug in place and they won't stumble. But they ignore you and keep entering through the back door. On several occasions they trip and skin themselves. It has been said, we are all creatures of habit. Certainly this was the case with early Jewish Christians.

This chapter makes the case for believers to forget their sins and move on. That is assuming they have addressed them before the Lord. Hanging on to guilt is not what Scripture teaches. If we confess our sin to God, we need never think of it again. Jesus' sacrifice for you was personal and permanent. Your sins, past, present and future are forgiven. Be mindful however, sin's consequences still remain. Don't become victim to sin's deceitfulness and test God by using Grace as a license to sin.

Animal sacrifice served as a temporary way to atone for sin until real forgiveness took place at the Cross. Sacrificing a <u>prized animal</u> impressed upon the individual God's worthiness and the cost of sin. Most importantly, God desired a contrite heart for sin and not just a *going through the motions* of sacrificing a bull.

The sitting aside of the Old Testament sacrificial system in no way set aside the Ten Commandments. They remain in force. The only thing that is changed is the manner of forgiveness for breaking them.

This observation of verse *twenty-six* may seem harsh as we relate it to the present day Church Age. To seemingly embrace the Church for a little while, even perhaps temporarily cleaning up one's act and singing *I Surrender All* a few times is useless if an individual ultimately becomes re-entangled in unabated sin. Scripture is clear. This is akin to a dog returning to his vomit. Proverb 26:11, 2 Peter 2:22

Application

Christ is solid ground! With Christ written on our heart and mind, we may enter with confidence the Holy of Holies. *"Let us hold unswervingly to the hope we profess, for He who promised is faithful."* (v. 23) But let us not be ignorant of the warning of verse twenty-six. This verse relates to being *"born again."* (John 3:3) Being born again displays <u>evidence of ongoing Christlikeness being born daily</u>, weekly, monthly in the individual. This evidence can be seen and experienced by others! Beloved, if there is no evidence of Spiritual leading, no matter what the person's lips say, unless his works match his lips, he is a liar and a hypocrite. See Romans 8:9, Revelation 2:2 (NKJV)

Enrichment Reading

Read Leviticus 18:24-30

Notes for Hebrews 10

HEBREWS 11
Faith's Hall of Fame

This chapter is the Bible's Hall of Fame of Old Testament Saints of Faith. Their stories, their resilience, challenge all who profess the Faith to trust the Lord in all areas of life. This chapter informs us that faithful men and women experience differing results; sometimes good, sometimes tragic. We know this to be especially true in the early Church. But ultimately, all share the same end result, God's Kingdom plan.

The individuals in this chapter have been evaluated. Their examples are recorded, not so much for our admiration, but to cultivate our trust of God in <u>all areas</u> of our lives.

Read Hebrews 11:1-31
1) a. Select a nonbiblical endeavor and name three people to its hall of fame.

    b. What qualifies them?

2) In a word, what is faith? _____ (Starts with letter A)

3) How is faith described in verse one?

4) What determines if faith has solid assurance or if it is a foolish faith?

Discussion:
Why do we view the word of some people dependable and others not dependable?

5) Would you say faith is personal and if it is personal, what makes it personal?

6) a. What are some negatives of keeping secrets within marriage?

    b. What is more important in a marriage, love or trust?

7) In the workplace or in friendships, what does keeping one's word generate?

8) What kind image do chronic excuse makers create for themselves?

9) Though they are unaware, chronic excuse makers are exhibiting a kind of fruit. *"Every tree that does not bear good fruit is cut down and thrown into the fire. Thus, by their fruit you will know them."* (Matthew 7:19-20) From this verse, what kind of danger might chronic excuse makers be in? See [Luke 14:15-24]

10) How would others measure you in the;

   a. dependability department?

   b. reliability of your word?

   c. trustworthiness with their valuables?

11) Would you say with God, faithfulness goes hand in hand with dependability?

12) Why might God call some less knowledgeable individuals to His service?

13) What does verse six have in common with Matthew 7:7-8

14) Does Hebrews 11:13, 35b-38 strike you as unfair and perhaps less trusting of God?

*Note: After writing your answer, check the Leader's Overview for insight to this verse.

15) The names and stories of these people would be familiar to Jewish converts. On a scale of zero to five, grade yourself how much you about each person.

Abel _____ Enoch _____ Noah _____ Abraham _____ Isaac _____ Jacob _____
Joseph _____ Moses _____ Rahab _____ Gideon _____ Barak _____
Samson _____ Jephthah _____ David _____ Samuel _____

Summary Statement:
Faith is *assurance* in One we view dependable and worthy of our trust.

Whether they believe it or not, all men will come before God by works or by faith. <u>Unbelief is the worst of sins because God has no remedy for it</u>! The unbelief that God even exists disables a man to believe the Word of God. The effect of this is like falling dominoes. They believe that happen-chance, not God, created all that is. They do not believe the existence of Heaven or hell. The things of God are meaningless. Think about it, unbelief denies both the Christ and the Holy Spirit. Such people are without hope. The unbeliever will neither humble himself nor seek forgiveness of sin he desperately needs.

Make note of the contrasts in the chapter beginning at verse thirty-two to the end. By faith some conquered kingdoms, administered justice and gained much from their efforts. By faith some quenched flames, shut the mouths of lions and escaped the sword. By faith some won battles, routed enemies, saw deceased sons restored back to life. (vv. 32-35a) Contrasts the tragic accounts of flogging, imprisonment, stoning, being sawed in two and living in destitute conditions. (vv. 35b-38) Beloved, it would be so wrong to dismiss their heartbreak simply as God testing their perseverance or strengthening their faith. Assuredly, they didn't see it that way.

To the contrary, these tragic accounts convey a great message. The end game is not the now, but rather the promise. Faith is unwavering whatever the circumstances! <u>Circumstances are not to determine faith</u>. To believe faith has a payout in this journey is contrary to the teachings of Jesus. [See John 15:18-25, Acts 9:16]

Biblical accounts of these individuals revealed all were flawed. Some resorted to lies and even murder. Abraham lied to the Egyptian Pharaoh to avoid certain death. Why does God choose flawed individuals to carry out His purpose? A look at the Apostle Paul answers this question. <u>Paul was deplorable but he was relentlessly dependable</u>. Like Abraham and the others, Paul could be trusted not to wilt. All of these people finished their respective purpose God set before them! None offered up excuses when the going got tough. We recall one excuse maker and what he missed out on. *"I will follow You Lord; but first let me go back and say good bye to my family."* (Luke 9:61) Beloved, dependability is a Christ like character trait that translates to being trusted by others not to wilt when confronted with obstacles. See John 4:31-34

Application

Faith is neither a matter of circumstances nor a thing for famous people. Faith is for all in everyday practical ways. How we work, make choices, meet trials, relate, think and especially wait! When faith is absent, in all cases, sin is not far behind!

Enrichment Reading

Read 1 Kings 17:17-24

Notes for Hebrews 11

HEBREWS 12
Shaping One's Life

Would anyone run a race loaded down with a backpack filled with rocks? Some commentators suggest Christians do exactly that! They cite believers seeking forgiveness for sins in general but refuse to acknowledge specific sins because they are too comfortable in them. Often, these are <u>sins that define who they are as a person</u>. British Bible Scholar, G. Campbell Morgan writes; *"We cry too often to be delivered from the punishment instead of the sin that lies beneath it. We are anxious to escape from the things that cause us pain rather than from the things that cause God pain."*

Read Hebrews 12:1-13

1) From verse one, what kind of race do you think the writer is alluding to for his readers to finish?

2) Whether you are not old enough to vote or you are a grandparent, if you are a believer, you are a child of God. What is the mind of God in regard to chastisement of His children presented in these verses? See also Proverbs 13:13, 24

3) What things does a child learn from the discipline of godly parents beginning with the one thing most important?

4) a. Name some of the fruit of a disciplined life? Include verse eleven.

   b. Name some of the fruit of an undisciplined life?

5) Verse four indicates the Romans had not yet destroyed the Temple. What were these Christian Jews still doing at that time that was useless to atone for their sins?

Discussion: First read Luke 15:20-24

Being at odds with others is more problematical than being at odds with God. God joyfully opens His arms to anyone who wishes to make peace with Him. From the Parable of the Prodigal Son, what is modeled when an estrangement is reconciled?

Read Hebrews 12:14-24

6) What does Romans 12:17-19 say in regard to being at peace with other people?

7) What does Romans 5:1 say in regard to being at peace with God?

8) Sexually immoral appears in the NIV Bible in relation to Esau in verse sixteen. A better translation for sexual is fornication because our subject here is about unfaithfulness to God, not illicit sexual behavior. Question, what was more important to Esau than being faithful to the birthright God had given him by his being born minutes ahead of Jacob? See Genesis 25:31-33

Discussion:

As a Christian, you are comfortable with the name Jesus. But have you ever felt cut off from family, people at work or neighbors because the J Word makes them uncomfortable? How do you deal with this? What should you do?

9) How might Christian Jews living in first century Jerusalem have been received in and about the Jewish Synagogues?

Read Hebrews 12:25-29

10) The New Testament identifies faith as a marathon to be finished. What goals are worth finishing and what things are we doing that is simply rocks in our back pack?

11) In what ways does your worship reflect or fail to reflect that you are in awe that your "Creator is a consuming fire?

Summary Statement:

The defining statement of Scripture is found in verse fourteen; *"without holiness no one will see the Lord." Holiness* starts first with believing that God exists! Second, embracing the provision of His Grace. And finally, the Son satisfied the sacrificial requirements of the Law given at Mount Sinai.

The previous chapter revealed inspiring examples of names etched forever in the pages of Scripture. Their names testify to the value of faith. Those individuals and the names of countless others of faith are written in still another book, The Lamb's Book of Life. Beloved, if you are a man or woman of faith, you can trust your name appearing in this most important of all books.

This chapter relates to the value and significance of the Lord's discipline. When we observe the arrogant, the world's takers, going about their business unimpeded soaking up what this life has to offer, know this. <u>That is all they are going to get!</u>

God has not disciplined them. What parent disciplines somebody else's child? An undisciplined man or woman is not a child of God. This is why the wicked so freely do the things that delights their father, the devil. Beloved, they need our prayers rather than our consternation! They are lost souls, dying in their lust for the pleasures worldly people treasure.

Knowing the destiny of the undisciplined, the writer asks God's people not to engage a life of whining and complaining about things they don't have. Others will think you envy those who have all the world's abundance. Christians must never convey God is holding them back. <u>Beloved, the things of God determine our abundance</u>. It doesn't get any better than having God's Word in our heart! *"Your Word is a lamp to my feet, a light for my path."* (Psalm 119:105) Christ's sacrifice released us from being judged by our own righteousness. What more is there to want? Our response to such love must include not bemoaning any lack of the world's pleasures.

Verse eighteen begins a reminder of the giving of the Law at Mount Sinai. God seemed distant, even terrifying to the people of the Exodus. God was only approachable through a priest and only then at the Tent of Meeting with an animal offering requirement. In Jesus, God has become directly approachable any place, any time, by anyone seeking Him. The only offering needed is one's self! (Romans 12:1) Because of Jesus, Mount Sinai is replaced by the Holy City, referenced here as Zion. A huge change has taken place. *"For my yoke is easy and my burden is light."* (Matthew 11:30)

It is interesting to note that at the giving of the Law, three thousand unfaithful Israelites died in their sin of unbelief. (Exodus 32:27-28) At the giving of the Holy Spirit at Pentecost, three thousand from all nationalities were born again by their believing faith. (Acts 2:1-12)

Application

The Lord's discipline comes to every child of God. Pray for God's strength to assist you in unloading any rocks in your backpack.

Enrichment Reading

Read Exodus 32:1-35, Acts 2:1-12

"The Road to Character" by David Brooks

This book presents two kinds of individuals, Adam I and Adam II. Adam I is a taker. Adam II is a giver. Adam I seeks to get the better of you. Adam II seeks to give you the better of himself. You get the picture. Adam II is a child of God and the treasures of Heaven await him. Adam I, not being a child of God, is extracting up all the treasures he can get out of this world while he can. "The Road to Character" is a must read. It has the potential to be a life changer for some and an encourager for those whose life has changed.

Notes for Hebrews 12

HEBREWS 13
Let Us Gather Together

The first ten chapters are the doctrinal chapters of the Epistle to the Hebrews. Chapters eleven, twelve and thirteen are the application of the first ten. Paul's Epistle to the Romans has much the same format. Romans 1-8 is the flagship of Christian Doctrine with Romans 12-16 its application. Truly be aware of this in Bible study.

Hebrews 11 was the Faith chapter. Chapter 12 defined one's hope as a child in the family of God. In this chapter, core relational teachings of Christ is addressed. *"Love one another as I have loved you."* (John 13:34) This verse suggests Christians live a life in fellowship with other believers rather than withdrawing and living like a hermit.

1) a. Verse nine embraces identifying things of value and things of little value. Name three things of significant value and why they are significant?

   b. Do you think God agrees or disagrees with your selections? Why?

Discussion: First read Galatians 5:16-26
What is missing in the character of the individual who puts on their church face publically, but back inside the home they are unsettled as Proverb 29:11 describes?

2) What is the city that is to come? (v. 14) See Revelation 21:1-4

3) a. What is the purpose of hymn singing?

   b. What might be tactfully said to encourage individuals who believe hymn singing is for others but not themselves?

   c. What are common excuses for not singing hymns? Are they valid?

4) What does verse seventeen say about leaders?

5) Disrespecting or *undermining leaders* reveals a rebellious nature. What does 1 Samuel 15:23, Romans 13:1-2, Numbers 16:1-2, 32-33 say about a rebellious heart?

Note: Those who listen to fractious media or engage in spreading internet hate of leaders are vulnerable to the devil or even possible Judgment. This is why the account of Korah's sin is in the Bible. Duly <u>elected officials have Divine Authority</u>. But elected officials are under Divine Authority. *"Woe in the world because of the things that cause people to sin! Such things must come, but woe to the man through whom they come!"* (Matthew 18:7) The makers of pornography, violent video games, and easy kill weapons to name a few, are gateways leading others into sin. For them, Scripture is clear, the fires of hell await them!

6) Opposing a leader is a perilous thing. But Scripture does offer insight on the subject. Daniel opposed King Darius (Daniel 6:6-10) and Peter defied authorities. (Acts 4:18:18-21) How did these two men respond to the mandates of an ungodly leader?

7) It is worthy to keep in mind that leaders in one area are followers in another area. When that occurs, what must a person accustomed to leading guard against?

Discussion:
Taking a back seat is difficult for some who are accustomed to being front and center. When this happens, arguably, God is testing that person in what respects?

8) The author of Hebrews is assuredly a leader in the early Church. What is it that he requests his Christian brothers and sisters to do for him? (vv, 18-19)

9) Not that it is important, but compare verse twenty-three with 1 Timothy 1:1-2 and make a guess about who the author of Hebrews might be?

10) What three things does the writer remind his readers of in verse twenty?

11) What will Jesus do for all who embrace Him with steadfast faith? (v. 21)

Summary Statement:
God's work in the believer is a result of the *blood* of the New Covenant.

We gather together to ask the Lord's blessing.

Something extraordinary has occurred! A mystery is revealed. Through the Lord Jesus, Gentiles and Jews have been brought together into a unifying bond. They have become brothers in Christ. Had the above hymn been available in the early Church, it could have been appropriately used as a unifying tool to encourage brotherly love between very diverse cultures.

For centuries, the Jews had claimed God for themselves. At the onset of Christianity, Jewish converts endeavored to hold to old ways of requiring such things as circumcision of the Gentiles and restrictive diets. The Apostle Paul addressed these issues consistently. Recall these verses, *"For the kingdom of God is not a matter of eating and drinking."* (Romans 14:17) *"Some men came down from Judea to Antioch and were teaching the brothers; 'Unless you are circumcised, according to the custom taught by Moses, you cannot be saved.'"* (Acts 15:1) Imagine the conflicts that would have existed in the early Church. Therefore, it should not be surprising there was a need for repetitive calls to *love one another.*

In Scripture, angels served as God's messengers. Therefore, you and I should be eager to welcome those speaking the name Jesus. In welcoming them, it is good to know the Bible. *"Watch out for false prophets. They come to you in sheep's clothing, but inwardly they are ferocious wolves. By their fruit you will know them."* (Matthew 7:15-16) If they eventually reveal an agenda that glorifies something or someone other than God, beloved, they are not who they say they are.

Application

Consistently gather with other believers; one small enough to know its leaders personally. Be personable with them, helpful and pray for them. If you go to a mega-church, join one of the smaller groups most mega-churches make available. Guard against God only knowing you as a Sunday morning pew warmer. The Holy Spirit was first given to a group, highlighting Church as a Body. (Acts 2:1-4)

"For where two or three come together in my name, there am I with them."

Matthew 18:20

Enrichment Reading

Read Numbers 16:1-35

Notes for Hebrews 13

Twenty Lessons
The Letters of

James, Peter,

John, Jude

ABOUT THE LETTERS OF JAMES, PETER, JOHN AND JUDE

This study is the <u>eyewitness account</u> of men who had a direct relationship with Jesus. After the Savior completed His earthly ministry, these men, with the addition of Paul, became Apostles. (One who is sent) Paul was the principal Apostle to the Gentiles. (Romans 11:13) See Also Acts 15:7 Divinely inspired, these men wrote with the hope their readers would come to understand that Jesus was God Incarnate, who had come to save men from the coming Judgment! *"He who has an ear let him hear."* (Revelation 2:11)

The Apostle James paints a portrait of a genuine Christian. The Faith that saves is confirmed by how trials are handled, follow-through is completed and the fingerprint of words left behind. Saving Faith produces works that are visible! Forensics would call this evidence. James offers practical advice even the most recent of converts can comprehend. A half-brother of Jesus, James (there were four James) was not one of the original twelve but later he was a principal leader in the Church at Jerusalem. His letter centers on <u>being what we claim to be</u> by doing the things Christians do.

The Apostle Peter established his sending at the Council at Jerusalem to be the spokesperson bridging the divide between Jews and Gentiles. (Acts 15:7-8) The account of his relationship with Jesus is given in the Gospels. Peter's letters are not idealistic in that, they speak on subjects of suffering, persecution and courage in the face of seemingly hopeless circumstances, Still, he comes across as one full of hope.

The Apostle John like Peter, experienced a close relationship with Jesus. His account is also related in the Gospels. John's letters were in response to the false teachings of the Gnostics; <u>a less than moral crowd</u> that nevertheless <u>associated themselves within the Christian community</u>. We see that today in the form of wolves in sheep's clothing who apparently think if they sleep in the garage they can masquerade as a car. Principally however, John relates to his readers the security they have in Christ.

Jude wished also to address the subject of security in Christ but was compelled to warn Christians of the <u>imposters within</u>. Today's Church is so overly focused on the <u>geopolitical enemies outside</u> and abortion-gay issues, it virtually ignores the frauds within. The apostate church and the wolves of the airwaves masquerading as part of the Community of Faith are hardly winked at in today's sermon topics.

Positioned just ahead of The Book of Revelation, Jude's letter is Scripture's final warning to be alert!

JAMES 1
Growing to Christian Maturity

Being saved is only the beginning! To finish the work of new birth involves growing pains. <u>These trials come for our good so we are to be joyful in them.</u> The mature Christian prayerfully communions with the Lord to see them through when trials do come. Communion develops a solid root. (Luke 8:5-8) As we grow closer to Christ, our ability to serve others in their time of difficulty increases. All to the glory of God.

The chapter ends with a declaration that hearing the Word and doing the Word go hand in hand. For instance, love is an appealing word. But until it is jump-started to action, love is simply just a pretty word.

Read James 1:1-12

1) What would you say about a teen who ate Gerber's for his meals and received his milk via a baby bottle?

2) Using Romans 12:1-2 as a model, how would you describe;

   a. an immature Christian?

   b. a mature Christian?

3) What is the message of verses nine and ten?

4) Write your reaction to this saying of an unknown author.

> *Is there no other way open, Lord,*
> *Except through sorrow, pain and loss,*
> *To stamp Christ's likeness on my soul?*

5) Though it may at times be gloomy, even hopeless, what awaits those who maintain their faith? (v. 12)

Time Out: Think on Hebrews 11:35b-40. On earth, things did not end well for these individuals of faith. So what sustained them? They simply were not invested/focused on this world but in the world to come when Christ our Lord gathers His sheep. <u>This is the perseverance of which James speaks.</u>

6) The *Crown of life* is addressed here. (v 12) Scripture identifies four other crowns. Crowns do not save, but they do relate to good works. Learn about them.

    a. What work is identified in 1 Corinthians 9:24-27?

    b. What work is identified in 1 Thessalonians 2:19?

    c. What work is identified in 1 Peter 5:1-4?

    d. What work is identified in 2 Timothy 4:6-8?

7) Scripture assures us that once saved always saved. Salvation cannot be lost because Jesus does not lose even one from His flock. (John 10:27-30) But in regard to crowns, what does 2 John 1:8 and Revelation 3:11 say?

Read James 1:13-21
Reflection: There are a lot of folks who get up every morning having no thought of the Lord and certainly no thought of doing anything to glorify His name during the day. What are some things you like to do to glorify His name? (Include the subject of anger)

8) What is the message of Romans 12:1-2?

Read James 1:22-27
Self-Examination: If your love and faith were placed under a microscope, what stage of maturity would be revealed? Baby, Adolescent, Teen, Young Adult, Mature Adult.

9) What is the message of Matthew 7:20-23?

10) Many attach religion to regular church attendance, Bible study, sermons, faith and love. But James expands religion to include what three principals? (vv. 26-27)

Summary Statement:
Once one has received Christ, the real work begins! The road to maturity leads in many directions, not the least being, how one develops in times of testing. Suffice to say, faith without corresponding evidence exposes one to being a pretender.

This chapter is multi-themed. But how James ends the chapter is the central point. To move Christianity from the comfort of our pews and out into the sorrows of the world. James calls for you and me to be more hands-on than simply dropping a few dollars in a disaster offering as we exit the Sanctuary. Certainly monetary gifts are needed and indeed, they make us feel noble. But this alone cost us little, really! One's time is the greater sacrifice. (View Application before going further)

To identify James' words in the perspective of today, we would say giving time and money to the church while ignoring one's aging parent is one example of useless religion. Paul calls such giving Corban and is worse than being an unbeliever. (1 Timothy 5:8) It befits us as Christians to not wait for somebody else to assist a neighbor in need of a hot meal or a pickup after surgery.

One of the great tragedies in the development of a child's character are parents that never expose their children to the needs of the elderly, even elderly family members. If a child doesn't develop empathy early, don't expect much out of them later.

The lack of empathy is a world-wide problem and the root cause so many suffer. Certainly, selfish thrill seekers, predators and violent men lack empathy and cause great suffering. Such men live as the beasts live. They have more in common with animals than humanity. But God's people are set apart (Sanctified) to rise above the instincts of beasts and perform works that glorify the Lord. For that reason, God's people cannot demonstrate indifference or ignorance where there is a need.

How many of us would go to the Lord in prayer if no trials ever came our way? When is the last time you cried for mercy? Do we get the picture why we are to take joy in trials? God notices us and He wants us to notice Him. Beloved, we are blessed when God wants us to communicate with Him! In trials and testing, God is about the business of maturing our faith, making us like His Son if you will! You see, Faith, like all muscles, needs to be exercised! Remember, God tested His own Son. (Matthew 16:1 and Hebrews 2:18)

James' goal in this Epistle is centered on how works identifies faith. If forensics don't reveal a heart of, and for the Savior, such a person is not a disciple of Jesus. *"No one can see the kingdom of God unless he is born again."* (John 3:3) These words of Jesus address the issue of regeneration or a type of *first fruit*. A new life replaces the old. The fruit of regeneration is *life*. The fruit of an unregenerate man is *death*.

Going forward, James' Epistle is a down to earth look into the forensics of Faith.

Application

No better conclusion could be written to this chapter than one written by J. Vernon McGee. A young boy had lost his mother. With her income now gone, the father's menial job provided little. Wanting more for his son, the father made arrangements with a wealthy relative to take the boy in. There the boy would have a new bicycle and the best of toys. He would get to travel and see things. His Christmas would be like none the boy had ever known. "They will do things for you that you would not have with me" said the father. But the little boy said, "I don't want to go." "Why not said the father?" "They can't give me you!"

Beloved, receiving Christ is not the end journey. It is the beginning of making one's self available to those who need you.

Notes for James 1

JAMES 2
Christianity is not a Spectator Faith – Do Something!

Genuine Faith doesn't flinch at sacrifice. Be it time or money, people who are the real deal pitch in where there is a need. <u>Genuine Faith surrenders personal appetites that bring harm to others</u>. *"Do nothing out of selfish ambition. Each of you should look not only to your own interests, but also to the interests of others."* (Philippians 2:3-4) Genuine Faith <u>does more</u> than observe a minute of silence following a tragedy. Genuine Faith <u>does more</u> than engage photo-opt tributes to victims. You and I would be in a real fix if all Jesus had done was observe a minute of silence at the Cross followed by an opportunistic speech. Christ got up on that Cross and died!

Read James 2:1-13

1) How does it make you feel to be marginalized as being unworthy? What are your feelings towards the people who deliberately slight you?

2) Identify the three arguments James gives against showing favoritism to the upper class.

   a. (vv. 5-7)

   b. (vv. 8-11)

   c. (vv. 12-13)

Discussion:
What do you think motivates people to show favoritism?

3) In what ways is favoritism manifested at the highest levels of Government?

4) In what ways is favoritism manifested in the daily lives of the working class?

5) Can favoritism be an innocent act or is it always sin in the eyes of God? Explain!

6)   What is the message of Proverbs 30:7-10?

7)   In what ways might one's apparel at a worship service be an affront to Christ?

Read James 2:14-26

8)   What two essentials does this passage from Hebrews reveal? *"By faith the people passed through the Red Sea. By faith the walls of Jericho fell, after the people had marched around them for seven days. By faith the prostitute Rahab, because she welcomed the spies, was not killed."* (Hebrews 11:29-31)

9)   Define faith; See Hebrews 11:1

10) Reconcile Hebrews 11:1 with James 2:18-19

11) Do you think one's will is an affecter of action? _____

12) When we do take an action, how should our attitude be? See Philippians 2:5

Summary Statement:

J. Vernon McGee's summation for this chapter is appropriate. Rahab disregarded herself in her service to the Lord. She did not stand-by singing *Praise God from whom all blessings flow* while the Israelite spies fended for themselves. She did not recite *Jesus saves.* She did not say *Hallelujah praise the Lord and fling her hands skyward!* The Bible doesn't even record a prayer. She simply got involved!

> *"Let your light shine before men,*
> *that they may see your good deeds*
> *and praise your Father in heaven."*
>
> **Matthew 5:16**

<u>Favoritism has two victims</u>. Yes, we try to hide it. But all of us have shown favoritism. Clearly, our Lord does not wish for His people to practice favoritism. Doubtless, favoritism does more harm to the one favored than the one granting the favor. In children, chronic favoritism can instill a sense of entitlement that lingers into adulthood. Chronic favoritism is a Spiritual death sentence. The entitled person thinks God owes him heaven because he is just so wonderful. Harm is also done to victims of favoritism. Over time, they withdraw into a feeling of diminished self-worth. A mind-set where any number of things can result; none of which glorify God. <u>When continual favoritism occurs in adults, this invariably leads to irreparable relationship damage</u>.

In the business world, favoritism is a form of nepotism. Individuals are granted positions they have neither earned or, are they qualified to hold. When that occurs, everyone suffers; those subordinate to that person and the customers themselves. Worse, those who excel are discouraged and say to themselves; "what's the use, I am never going to be treated fairly." Absolutely, favoritism is not a minor thing!

Works of faith must cost us something to glorify God. A sacrifice has to be made!

Changing a tire for an elderly person or taking a hot meal to a neighbor who is ill cost us time and money. Volunteer work or financially assisting a need requires a sacrifice. Anytime *goodness* is engaged, the *fruit of the Spirit* is demonstrated.

A man cannot say he is a believer while his lack of action serves the devil.

A man can be doing the most for the devil when he is doing nothing! Repeat; A man can be doing the most for the devil when he is doing nothing. There is no more glorious example of this than in our Nation's Capital. Men, women, children and public servants are being murdered by the tens of thousands and the best those who could do the most is observe a minute of silence and appear distressed on camera. <u>On this subject the Church is strikingly silent</u>! Many lips speak of Christ but their inaction tells a different story. *"He never knew you."* (Matthew 7:15-23, 25:45-46)

Using a broader brush, <u>feeding the appetites of the flesh</u> are ungodly works. For example, purchasing homes, cars, clothes or vacations we can't afford are ungodly works. Though our lips may say Jesus, our materialism says He *never knew you.*

How we spend our leisure time and money speaks volumes as to our authenticity. We can't recite the Christmas story to our children and place mystic storybooks and violent video games under the Christmas tree. We cannot be attending church retreats while secretly subscribing to internet pornography. Or can we be visiting topless lounges and opposing abortion clinics while harboring an arsenal of weapons in our closets. Morality cannot be a matter of personal appetite.

> *"Do not be deceived," God cannot be mocked.*
> *A man reaps what he sows,"*
> *"The one who sows to please his sinful nature,*
> *from that nature will reap destruction."*
>
> Galatians 6:7-8

Two-Fold Application

"Foxes have holes and birds of the air have nests, but the Son of Man has no place to lay his head." (Matthew 8:20) In every respect, Jesus was slighted. Therefore, being slighted puts you in good company. On the flipside, when we slight another person, are we not in essence, slighting the Savior Himself? Slighting another is in effect, a carbon copy of Matthew 25:45-46. *"I tell you the truth, whatever you did not do for one of the least of these, you did not do for me." "Then they will go away to eternal punishment, but the righteous to eternal life."*

Genuine faith requires some degree of sacrifice, either time, money or a rejection of the desires of the flesh.

Notes for James 2

JAMES 3
The Power of Words

"Set a guard over my mouth, O Lord, keep watch over the door of my lips." (Psalm 141:3) This Psalm of David is the center-fold of this chapter. A reading of Matthew 26:73 reminds us that the tongue reveals whether one is educated, cultured or crude, negative or positive, vulgar or refined, humble or full of self. <u>There is a fetter connecting the tongue back to the heart</u>. This chapter concludes, if the heart is pure, the tongue will reveal an individual controlled by the Holy Spirit.

"Blessed are the pure in heart, for they will see God."

Read James 3:1-12

1) How might the tongue relate to Matthew 7:22-23?

2) a. Name the five parts of the body identified in Proverbs 6:16-19 that represent one being taken into sin if not under the control of the Spirit of God?

   b. Which of the sins are identified that the tongue is the principal contributor?

3) What is James' warning to those who teach or otherwise have positions where-by they are an influence on other individuals?

4) What is the message of Matthew 18:7.

5) What benefit does James place on the person whose tongue is under control?

6) a. What power guides horses and ships? _____ (v. 3)

   b. If the human power is disordered, what is the source of power? (vv. 14-15)

7) What is the alarming message of verses five and six?

8) What does James say concerning both fresh water and salt water coming from the same spring?

9) How might God and a forensic scientist do similar work? See Ecclesiastes 12:14

Read James 3:13-18

Discussion:
Scripture tells us the devil is behind all envy and selfish ambition. (vv. 14-15) So why might people who are aware of this still insist on displaying these ungodly attributes?

10) What are the expressions of a Christ-like person? See Galatians 5:22-26

Discussion:
What are some dangers of running for political office or even working in that arena?

11) Considering Jesus' words in Mark 9:43-47, what would you say to a friend who works in a political campaign or any occupation where character assassination and deception is not only common, it is expected?

Discussion:
Do you think social media should be included as parallel to sins of the tongue?

12) We know what it is to bare false witness about others. So then, how do you define one who is mendacious about self?

Summary Statement:
James exhorts the Church to use wisdom when speaking. For it is the mission of the Church to avoid divisiveness and ugliness when interacting with others.

With words, Creation came into existence. (Genesis 1:1, 3, 6, 9, 11, 14, 20, 24, 29, 2:18, John 1:1) Beloved, words have power! God used words to make good things. Unfortunately, the words of men and women don't always make for good things.

"As a man speaks, so he is!" (Matthew 26:73) It isn't any surprise to find individuals outside the Faith telling lewd jokes and using expletives to describe every other noun. <u>Saving Faith</u> is displayed when the follower of Christ doesn't engage lewd talk even when in the company of those who do.

<u>Saving Faith</u> is not just a matter of singing "Praise God from whom all blessings flow" or avoiding vile verbiage. When James speaks of disorder and evil practices, <u>he is using a broader brush</u>. Half-truths and outright lying has led some countries to war. Innuendo and gossip purposely take others down. Any of us can become a character assassin if we are not controlled by the Spirit of God. The sole purpose of a character assassin is to gain advantage by damaging the character of another. When we find ourselves debasing another, we need to ask our self, what is our motive here? Irresponsible words are the work of the devil, James explains.

Character assassination more often than not is displayed in the political arena. The reason is obvious, to gain an advantage. Wouldn't it be lovely if candidates spoke only of their worthiness rather than the unworthiness of their opponents? Trickery is the principal ingredient in many political campaigns. Some of these people will say anything about others to get elected. Sadly, political character assassination finds its way into Bible study classes when <u>teachers are asleep at the wheel</u>. Leaders not only have the obligation to teach the Gospel of Christ accurately, they must curb divisiveness the devil's tongue can bring into the Christian arena.

"God has not given us a spirit of fear, but of power and of love and of a <u>sound mind</u>." (2 Timothy 1:7 NKJV) In our technological age, social media is an extension of our tongue. The Media itself, ever alert to ratings that drive their fees, find fanning the fires of fear and discord more profitable than any other subject. When we fly the banner of Jesus, be it face to face or social media, let us not be sailing under false colors. One writer put it this way:

> Don't be one who will be clutching his Bible at the gates of hell.

Application

As a fingerprint reveals the identity of a person, so also a word-print identifies the character of a person.

The tongue is the press secretary for the heart just as the White House Press Secretary is the spokesperson for the one in the oval office. Our tongue is our own personal press secretary. Let Jesus occupy the oval office of your heart?

The tongue that confesses Christ should not be a tongue denying that confession.

Notes for James 3

JAMES 4
The Absence of Intimacy

It is right for the Church to be in the world;
It is wrong for the world to be in the Church.
Harold Lindsell

Where intimacy is absent, sin is not far behind! *"I, the Lord your God, am a Jealous God."* (Exodus 20:5) This pretty much is the point of this chapter. God is not in the business of sharing one's devotion with the idols of this world. Unfortunately, many who claim God don't really understand the concept. They take privilege in reciting His name, <u>but they don't belong to Him</u>. They belong to the world. (John 8:47) Simply put, intimacy with God is absent. God is merely a conduit, a prop if you will, to feel godly and create the perception of godliness.

When the world gets mixed in with the Church, conflicts occur between those who belong to God and those who belong to the world. This is what James is addressing. This is why Jesus said He came to divide. (Luke 12:51) With conflict comes the fruit it produces, bitterness. James calls for unity of Spirit by putting God in first place.

Do not <u>confuse worldliness with sin</u>. They are two different subjects. *See Overview

Read James 4:1-10 Positioning God in our life

1) a. How might it be possible for two people to faithfully attend the same church yet don't so much as even speak to one another?

   b. How might it be possible for a married couple, living in the same house remain separated souls?

   Note: Consider being separated in spirit.

2) Describe and compare an un-invested spouse with an un-invested Christian.

3) Concerning Christ, what is Jesus' message to the Church at Ephesus? See Revelation 2:2-5

4) What is the message of Luke 14:26?

5) Unfaithfulness doesn't always have to do with sex. To what type of unfaithfulness is James addressing in verse four?

6) How is verse seven representative of the principles of the covenant of marriage?

Discussion:
In your words, what is double-mindedness and why is this condition not desirable?

7) How do James and Paul echo the same message? See Galatians 5:24-26

Read James 4:11-12 – Judging Others
8) What is the message of John 5:22-23?

Discussion:
There is no denying, we live in a dangerous world. How can we be discerning to personal danger without being judgmental?

Read James 4:13-17 – God's Will or Man's Will
9) In the totality of the big picture, how does Scripture describe the life of a human being? (v. 14) See Psalm 144:4

10) What is the life span of a man according to Psalm 90:10? _____

11) The Bible tells us life is short. But the Bible also tells us there is a way to make the most of the time given us. What does John 10:10b say on this subject?

Summary Statement:
~~The absence of intimacy with God serves ... placing God in a secondary~~ position makes one an adulterer and an enemy of God. (v. 4) The remedy is to draw near to God. (v. 8) It is not ours to judge other believers. The chapter concludes with a dialogue describing the limitations of men.

Time Out: Perhaps there is no other subject that presents serious issues in today's Church than the issue of music. The friction between the infusions of secular styled music into the Church has split many Congregations.

We will miss the point of this chapter if we try to put weaknesses of the flesh (sin) and worldliness (Idol worship) in the same basket. They are two entirely different issues! This chapter addresses knowing about God <u>but not belonging to Him</u>. Those occasional failures we call sin, of course, grieve the Spirit, but they <u>do not cost us our Salvation</u>. This chapter centers on the violation of the First Commandment; loving <u>the Creation more than the Creator</u>. This is the foolishness that will cost one his Salvation! Such faithfulness is to *self* rather than God.

How do we put God in first place? It starts with <u>putting self in second place</u>. That means, putting the things of God (Moral imperatives and the interest of others) ahead of the things that serve our personal appetites.

> *"Many live as enemies of the cross of Christ. Their destiny is destruction, their god is their stomach, their mind is on earthly things."*
> **Philippians 3:18-19**

We have unending quarreling over such issues as guns, abortion and gay marriage. Personal appetites is the driving force in all such quarreling rather than the Word of God. <u>Worldliness is not rooted in sin, it is rooted in selfishness.</u> (Me first) Of course, where selfishness is present, sin is not far behind. No cross displayed, no fish attached to a car, no amount of churchy activity can make amends for a selfish heart.

Keeping in mind, the Cross has both a vertical (Man's relationship to God) and horizontal branch, (Man's relationship to man) this chapter establishes the principal of <u>being invested whenever a Covenant exists</u>. The body of Christ carries a Covenant. To love one another. It shouldn't be too much a stretch to include the covenant of marriage. As to the former, Paul writes; *"Do nothing out of selfish ambition or vain conceit, but in humility, consider others better than yourselves. Each of you should look not only to your own interests, but also to the interests of others."* (Philippians 2:3-4) As to the latter, it is sin to position a pet, a career, a hobby, a close friend, in-laws, even children, grandchildren and church above one's <u>spouse with whom a Covenant exists</u>. To do so sends the same message worldliness sends to God, <u>you are unworthy to be number one</u>. If your spouse is little more than a prop, beloved, you are unfaithful. Jealously *is* a legitimate part of the vocabulary of love. (Exodus 20:5) Jealously is a normal reaction when first place subjects are given secondary positions. God Himself testifies to this.

Application

"Come near to God and he will come near to you." (v. 8) (The same can be said if we have a spouse.)

Until we can arrive at the point of longing for the Lord more than we long for the toys of the world and the entitlements of our mind, the devil will take the opportunity to play havoc in our lives and in our relationships.

Notes for James 4

JAMES 5
A Review

This chapter covers multiple subjects including the coming Judgment. We know the Epistles are directed to the Church. But the opening tone of this chapter makes it clear, not all who are churchy belong to God. This letter includes a continuation of the first ten verses of James 4, <u>worldliness</u>. If we translate the first six verses to today's world, we might certainly consider being such as a corporate lobbyist is fraught with peril.

Really, much of the Epistle of James is directed at the need to be aware there is a coming Judgment and God's people ought to remain alert. Belonging to God as opposed to claiming God is separated by the fruit of one's works. James concludes his Epistle on communion with God, specifically, the value of prayer.

> Sometimes we have to change our circumstances
> before our circumstances change us.

Discussion:

How might one's circumstances be a contributing factor to worldly living; the consequences being, Eternal Judgment?

Read James 5:1-6

1) What is the message of Matthew 6:24 and Luke 16:19-26

2) Money does not have to cost one his soul! Both Abraham and Job were wealthy by Old Testament standards. Besides extensive holdings, Job possessed wisdom. (See Job 1:1) How did Jesus' directive in Revelation 2:4 coincide with Job's wisdom?

3) What is the message of Revelation 3:17-22?

4) The subject of acquiring money by dishonest means is addressed in verse four. Besides law breaking such as armed robbery and selling drugs, name two lawful ways money is acquired but God would judge as shameful money.

5) Name a lawful industry that lobbies with the intent to profit from the manufacture and sales of instruments of mass murder?

Read James 5:7-12

6) To what event and circumstances does James ask of God's people to be patient?

7) While God's people patiently await the Second Coming of our Lord Jesus, what must the people of God avoid? (v. 9)

8) To what quality is Job a role model? See Job 1:6-22

Read James 5:13-20

9) Exhibitions of faith are unlimited. What does James advise his readers as to;

   a. trouble?

   b. happiness?

   c. illness?

   d. sin?

   e. Write down and memorize James 5:16b.

Summary Statement:

In the Church, hypocrisy and wealth can become bed-fellows if one is not alert. James also includes those who are always unhappy about something, the grumblers if you will! To both types this verse relates; *"Be self-controlled and alert. Your enemy the devil prowls around like a roaring lion looking for someone to devour. Resist him."* (2 Peter 8) James ends his Epistle on the value and power of *"the prayers of a righteous man."* (v. 16)

 **Leader's Helicopter Overview of James 5**
(Optional or Prepare Your Own)

*"Woe to him who builds his house by unrighteousness
And his chambers by injustice.* Jeremiah 13 NKJV

Evidently, church attendees in the South circa 1800s failed to read James 5. To draw a phrase from satire about the "Golden Rule," it goes like this; whoever has the gold makes the rules! The world honors those who are affluent but will God?

We know from Abraham, Job and other scriptural accounts of people of means, affluence is not condemned, but the love of it *is* condemned. James is not speaking to rich people outside the Church here, he is speaking to people in the Church who, nevertheless, are in the business of taking advantage of naïve and/or disadvantaged folks. One doesn't have to wield a gun or deal in drugs to acquire iniquitous money! There are too many schemes to name them all but we would be remiss not to consider some in hopes that <u>other parallels are drawn</u>. Condemning land owned by poor folks so that rich folks might profit or cheating a farmer out of oil-lease money comes to mind. Convincing elderly folks to send their social security checks in support of a ministry that is a ministry only in the sense they say all the right things and belong to the right political party. <u>Neither can we overlook industries that appeal to the base nature of humans of which the number is staggering</u>. Suffice to say, there are more iniquitous dollars earned than virtuous dollars. Worldly minds even prostitute the name of Jesus. But James promises them the fires of hell for ill-gotten riches. Assuredly, Jesus had schemers and oppressors in mind when He said; *"Not everyone who says to me, Lord, Lord, will enter the kingdom of heaven."* (Matthew 7:21)

Like the tongue in chapter three and strife in chapter four, being judgmental is not a Sanctified work in the Body of Christ. Judging people is the exclusive work of the Son. See John 5:22 Not knowing a man's heart, we ought not to be judging them.

*"First, take the plank out of your own eye and then you will see clearly
to remove the speck from your brother's eye."* Matthew 7:5

Time Out: We live in dangerous times. There are people who will play you or take advantage of your goodness to bring you harm. How can you temper prudence with not being judgmental?

It is fitting that James closes his Epistle on the subject of communion with the Lord. (Not the Lord's Supper) That is, any <u>activity that acknowledges that God exists.</u> This is accomplished when we look to Him for our provisions, most especially, to save us.

Application
The Existence of God

<u>It is good to ask things of God</u>. He wants us to do that. He knows He exists but He wants to hear us acknowledge that He exists. Much like your spouse knows you love them, but they want to hear it from you anyway. Not for them, but for you!

There are equally as many, if not more, Scriptures that offer opportunity to simply praise God without always besieging Him for some need. <u>Let us simply praise Him for who He is and what He has done.</u> Certainly, we should never be a spectator in hymn singing. One day praise and worship will be our daily routine. So let us be about the business of getting our singing praise chops in shape. And lastly, while we wait for the Second Coming of the Lord Jesus, remember patience. Maranatha!

"It is good that one would hope and wait quietly for the salvation of the Lord." (Lamentations 3:26)

Notes for James 5

1 PETER 1
At Rest in Christ

This chapter introduces the concept of election. More on this subject is taken up in the overview and addendum. *Hope* when used in the Bible is translated assurance. In Christ, Christians are assured of eternal life! But until that which is eternal comes to fruition, grief remains a part of life in the present world. Christians will find rest for their minds by being a forward-looking people to the world to come. Until such time, live holy lives.

Read 1 Peter 1:1-2

1) How does Peter identify a Christian in the present world?

2) What does it mean to be Sanctified? Use a Bible Dictionary if necessary.

3) What did God have a foreknowledge of that He Himself would have to fix? See Genesis 3:8-11, 17-19

4) What power gives man the ability to carry on with the work of Sanctification?

Read 1 Peter 1:3-12

5) By what attribute of God is Grace shed upon you and me? (v.3)

6) It has been observed that many Christians have little or no knowledge of God's attributes. His attributes are a part of the basics. Write down some attributes of God that come to mind. Let's start with:

He is <u>merciful</u>, He is _____, He is _____, He is _____

Can you think of more?

7) Verse five carries several promises. What are they?

8) What are the realities of a Christian living in the present world?

9) What does Peter say is the purpose of the grief and difficulties we endure? (v.7)

10) Even in the face of on-going trials and tribulation, on what should a believer remain focused?

11) Fulfilled Prophecy is an integral part of why the Christian Faith is the only religion on earth one can truly rely on as being genuine. One such prophecy was Isaiah 52:14-53:12. What was this Prophecy of Isaiah that came to pass?

Discussion:
What evidence do we have that Isaiah's prophecy about Christ actually occurred?

Read 1 Peter 1:13-25

12) Given God's merciful nature, He has saved us by Grace in the person of Jesus. In return for God's gift, what responsibilities should you and I assume? (v. 16)

13) Considering the flesh is weak, responsibilities seem like a tall order. What power has God given us to see us through? See John 14:16 and Acts 1:8

14) When we do stumble, even terribly, how do we know that God will not give up on us and give us over to Satan? See Matthew 28:20 and Hebrews 13:5

Discussion: Read Matthew 5:16
Sanctification relates to being *set apart* to do good works that glorify God. Justification occurred at the cross of Christ. When will Glorification occur? (v. 21)

Summary Statement:
In Christ, a Christian is a citizen of the Kingdom of Heaven and is a sojourner in a hostile land. The Christian life should not be shaped by the land in which he visits. Rather, they are shaped by the world they are assured is coming! If one is not a forward looking person, are they really a believer?

Peter introduces the subject of election. <u>Election appoints one to a new position.</u> Following one's election, governing becomes a duty. In the case of a Christian, governing one's own life responsibly. The Bible calls this Sanctification. Like all New Testament Epistles, Peter's letter is addressed to the Elect, the Church. The only part of the New Testament that is directed to unbelievers are the four Gospels.

Peter's subject of election is debated today among Theologians. Some suggest that before the foundations of the world, God elected some while others were to be denied. Some say Romans 9:15 suggests this conclusion, but the context here is Sovereignty. Revelation 3:5 indicates every name was entered in the book of life. Why? From the foundation of the world <u>it was God's plan to live in a relationship with His highest creation in an everlasting garden</u>. But given a freewill, man severed his relationship with God through disobedience. In mercy, God reached down to restore the break in the person of Jesus Christ. The Cross healed the relationship with New Testament individuals and retroactively restored Old Testament individuals who had believed God. (James 2:23)

If we connect John 3:16 and John 10:27, <u>the Spirit speaks to all men</u>, not just some men, calling all back into a relationship with the Father through the means He mercifully established, the person of Jesus. The problem is of the will. Some hear His voice while others harden their hearts. Folks, God doesn't send people to hell, they send themselves! They are given-over unto Judgment and their names are blotted out of the book of life. (Revelation 3:5) Those whose names remain in the Book are God's Elect and not as some say, were arbitrarily predestined. Predestination is biblical yes, but <u>it relates to a place, not a condition</u>.

Too often, Christians engage in useless arguing about predestination because one party confuses condition with predestination. They are not the same!

All of us are sheep! Sheep who respond to the Shepherd's call are the Elect. Sanctified, their purpose is to walk as citizens of heaven, obeying the Father's will and serve as God's workmen in a hostile world. The Elect are Justified before God by the Blood of Jesus. <u>Their Glorification is assured</u> and officially takes place at the Rapture of the Church. (1 Thessalonians 4:16-17) 2 Kings 5:1-15 relates a story that confirms, doing things God's way, good results.

Application

<u>Election involves governing.</u> A born again Christian assumes the position of governing a life; their own! They are mandated to govern their lives to the will of God rather than the will of the flesh. This is the call; *"offer your bodies as living sacrifices, holy and pleasing to God. No longer conforming to the pattern of this world, but be transformed by the renewing of your mind."* (pp. from Romans 12:1-2)

Additional Insight Addendum to 1 Peter 1

The Parables of the Wheat and the Weeds (Matthew 13:24-30) indicates not all within the Christian community are genuine. We are to be wary of those who govern their life in such a way that it is not distinguishably different from the world.

Election is a position change: New birth, new family, new citizenship, new guidance system controlled by the leading of the Spirit rather than the leading of the flesh. Everything is new! The greatest position change is one of <u>life replacing death</u>.

Election involves governing: Governing self responsibly to live a holy life! Election is available to all men: *"For God so loved the world."* This does not say 'God loved some of the world.' <u>Those who do not harden their heart to the calling of the Spirit,</u> <u>hear the Shepherds voice</u>. (John 10:27) These are the folks the Father elevates to a new position. (John 17:24) Their <u>election was predestined to be validated at the Cross</u>. (Justified)

To offer a different view, some suggest Matthew 7:13-14; John 6:44 and John 10:29 reveals that the Spirit does not call every man! Really? Does anyone ever say, "if the Spirit would call me I would go to Jesus?" Or does anyone ever say, "the Spirit called me but I told Him no?" So how can it be said, God only calls some? Could this not open the door to <u>elitist thinking, even boasting</u>?

All life IS precious in the sight of God. The Spirit calls everyone made in the image of God but few respond. Their obstinate hearts refuse to hear the Shepherd's voice simply because they are attuned to other voices. Their election/calling is defeated and they retain their old position! (Death) In the right context, Election, Predestination and Freewill are all true.

Predestination: God's Sovereign advance blueprint of a planned destination:
Sovereignty: God's will expressly exhibited in Deuteronomy 7 and Revelation 6-19

1 PETER 2
Who and What You Are In Christ

With election Justified, the job of governing our lives begins. Peter makes it clear, governing begins with development. Developing into a mature, <u>recognizable</u> Christian.

Read 1 Peter 2:1-12 – Read also 2 Timothy 2:15-16, 19-26

1) Define the following words and explain how they destroy character.

    a. malice:

    b. deceit:

    c. hypocrisy:

    d. envy:

    e. slander:

Which if any, do you identify as possible problem elements in your character?

2) Will diligent church attendance or Bible reading rid a person of these sins?

Discussion:

What do you think it means as a Christian to mature in your Faith? What are some things people do that have the appearance of growing in their Faith when in fact, no maturation progress has occurred at all?

3) Do you think little or no prayer life stagnates maturing as a Christian? What are the benefits of prayer?

4) If our prayer life is little to nothing, is that Satan's fault or our own?

5) Old Testament sacrifices consisted of animals. What is the New Testament spiritual sacrifice? See Romans 12:1

6) How is it that a Christian is a spiritual house?

Discussion:
Test your Old Testament savvy. How is it Christians are a Holy Priesthood? See Romans 12:2

7) Christ carries many names in the Bible. One of those metaphors is stone. How can the same stone be both a benefit and a stumbling stone?

8) Verse nine indicates who most likely Peter is ministering to. Identify them.

9) Who was it the Apostle Paul was assigned to minister to? See Romans 11:13

10) How does Peter identify Christian citizenship on earth? (v. 11)

11) What is the message to Christians today that verse twelve addresses? See Matthew 5:13-16

Read 1 Peter 2:13-25

12) According to verses thirteen through fifteen, what do you hear in today's world that Peter calls ignorant, irresponsible talk?

13) How much are you on board with antigovernment talk?

14) How is irresponsible (Ignorant) talk about government detrimental to a society?

15) What happens to the Gospel in a society constantly in turmoil with itself?

16) What do verses twenty and twenty-one tell us about Christian maturity?

17) What is Peter's description of all men? Consider even the Garden of Eden. (v. 25)

Summary Statement:
Christ suffered on behalf of the Elect. The Elect are to govern over a holy life.

Anytime a new section begins with 'therefore, examining the preceding material is obligatory! Not to do so nearly always results in missing the point of the new material. Because of election, this chapter is relevant to Chapter 1:1.

Peter speaks of maturing as a Christian. Nowhere is it suggested faithful church attendance and faithful Bible reading is the path to maturing. Sacrifice, even suffering he says, is the road to maturity. Certainly attending church and Bible study are essential to the Christian experience and aide in <u>governing our life responsibly.</u> Certainly maturity necessitates properly attending to relationships in the home and outside the home.

<u>Relationship with God:</u> This includes communion with Him thru prayer, worship, and gathering with other believers on a regular basis such as a weekly Bible study. Some believers seem to have forgotten, we were made for community. God's community is the Church for which He died! (Ephesians 5:25)

<u>Relationship with unbelievers:</u> The only Bible unbelievers experience is the behavior of God's people.

<u>Relationship with government:</u> Are you one who is quick to criticize people in office more than you pray for them?

<u>Relationship with superiors:</u> This would include teachers, workplace managers etc...

<u>Relationships with those who mistreat you:</u> This of course, is a tough one. But Peter reminds us, Jesus experienced mistreatment in that, He suffered punishment due us. When we suffer undue ridicule or malice, the manner we handle these things produces a fruit. Think of Saul and David. I think we should assume, God not only uses mistreatment to test the maturity of His people, He uses it to strengthen them.

<u>When God tests us</u>, the immature Christian produces the fruit of the flesh which is seeking revenge for mistreatment. If retaliation is your response to being wronged, you simply have not overcome the old nature, pride! When tested, the mature Christian will display the new nature. *"If it is possible, as far as it depends on you, live at peace with everyone."* (Romans 12:18)

This chapter begins with five works of the flesh, malice, deceit, hypocrisy, envy and slander. <u>Anyone of these on exhibit by a Christian demeans the Cross and is a mockery of the Faith</u>. One cannot sing *I Surrender All* on Sunday mornings and be actively practicing any of these qualities. *"Do not be deceived, God cannot be mocked. A man reaps what he sows, the one who sows to please his sinful nature, from that nature will reap destruction."* (Galatians 6:7-8)

Application

Suffering may be no more than giving up a place in line. Maturing is taking place every time we don't seek revenge for a wrong or when we refrain from trying to get the better of another person just because we can. This can be related to bullying. Bullying occurs because someone holds the upper hand either in position, wealth, physical strength, horse power or superior numbers. Even superior biblical knowledge can be a source of lording one's self over others.

Notes for 1 Peter 2

Journal for the Week

A. Relational Victory

B. Relational Challenges

C. Personal Victories

    a. Overcoming hidden sin or sin harmful to a family member or a friend.

    b. Bad Habit diminished, good one either started or sustained.

D. Personal Challenges

1 PETER 3
Marriage, Suffering, Christ

Husbands and wives are to govern their lives in relation to one another. The guiding principal is love, honor and respect. Apart from marriage, governing relationships with believers and nonbelievers is essential to satisfy the purpose of Sanctification.

Read 1 Peter 3:1-7

1) What does a kindly wife better accomplish with her unbelieving husband than would the wife who is in-his-face about the things of God?

2) All of us are either guided by the flesh or by the Spirit. What would you say of the woman who spends more time in front of the mirror than she does in the Bible?

3) What does Proverbs 31:10-12 tell a wife about governing herself in marriage?

4) What acts of nurturing might a husband practice to show love for his wife?

5) Which verse assures wives they carry the same election as their husband in regard to their position in God's family? _____

6) What does verse seven tell a husband about the effectiveness of his prayer life?

Discussion:

How might a fundamentalist husband misuse these biblical words, *weaker* and *submissive* in the marriage relationship?

Read 1 Peter 3:8-22

7) Verses eight through twelve are clear, relationships matter to the Lord! What must be governed to maintain harmonious relationships in marriage and in other relationships?

8) a. Who is more likely to retaliate against you, a believer or an unbeliever if you do something that displeases them?

 b. Why is this so?

9) Verse fifteen exhorts believers to know why Christ is Lord. What hard evidence do you have that Jesus is who He says He is? What evidence proves the Bible true?

Discussion:
How are Faith and hard evidence compatible?

10) Explain the difference between a soft touch and hitting an unbeliever over the head with your Bible.

11) Explain the difference in suffering for a good deed and suffering for having made a poor choice?

12) Why should you do the right thing when you know you will suffer repercussions for having done so?

13) By what power does Peter relate that the dead are raised to life?

14) Two Baptisms are identified in Scripture. What are they and how are they different? See Acts 1:5

15) What evidence is there to support verse twenty-two that Christ is indeed in Heaven? See Acts 1:1-9, Matthew 17:1-9, Revelation 1:12-18

Discussion:
Explain the role of secrets among friends about others. Explain the damage secrets can do within family when some members are included while another is excluded.

Summary Statement:
Multiple subjects are presented in this chapter. The key ones being the marriage relationship, suffering for godly deeds and the work and whereabouts of Christ.

It is possible to be a bit amused in this chapter. The principles of marriage is followed by expectations of suffering.

One of the more godly of character traits is least desired by most. Submission is hardly anyone's cup of tea because it suggests inferiority. It is unnatural and goes against the grain in a prideful world. But as we study the teachings of Jesus, He was often against the grain of the world's values. So it is no surprise <u>the Savior would be the one to demonstrate the value God places on submission</u>. Jesus demonstrated submission when he willingly, not grudgingly, went to the cross. The key word here is <u>willingly</u>. He obediently submitted Himself because the Father asked this of Him. (John 3:16) Submission was not easy for Jesus. Scripture describes the anguish He experienced prior to the cross. (Luke 22:42 Mark 14:35-36)

<u>Submission is not a sign of inferiority or weakness</u> in regard to God's commands. Christ never exhibited either quality and wives need not think they need too. The context for submission here <u>is for the sake of order in an institution</u>. In the military, submission runs from the army private to the oval office and it too, is subject to the electorate and congressional veto. <u>In marriage, a wife is to possess a quiet spirit</u>. A quiet spirit will move a husband to value his wife more than an in-your-face drama queen. <u>Husbands are not to take advantage of his wife's gentle nature.</u>

WHERE SUBMISSION IS ABSENT, TURMOIL ABOUNDS

You and I will never physically suffer nails being driven through our hands and feet. Still, we will suffer trials in life. In fact, God insists we do! So given the fact that <u>God deliberately sends trials, it is best we understand their purpose</u>. Faith requires exercise and training to run the race Sanctification requires. *"I have fought the good fight, I have run the race."* (2 Timothy 4:7) Trials perfect and strengthen faith just as exercise and training perfects and strengthens an athlete. If we consider faith a muscle, we can better understand the need to strengthen it.

"The lips of the righteous man speaks wisdom, his tongue is just."

Psalm 37:30

<u>Verse fifteen is one of the Bible's key verses to witnessing</u>. If a believer ask why you trust Christ as your Savior and your answer is your faith in Him, the answer is satisfactory. If an unbeliever ask the same question, a different answer is needed. They want evidence! So, remember, your own faith is based on immutable evidence.

That evidence is fulfilled Prophecy and eyewitness accounts of those who walked with Jesus during His ministry. They witnessed His miracles, His Glorification, His Resurrection and His Ascension. Everything He spoke aligned with the Prophets, proving he wasn't a liar. Who says Faith is blind?

Time Out: For some, unbelief and skepticism of who Jesus was is not really unbelief or skepticism but a matter of the will, pride if you will. <u>They just are not willing to bend their knees</u> because submission denies self. *"If anyone would come after me, he must deny himself and take up his cross daily and follow me."* (Luke 9:23) <u>Such a person requires a different kind of witness from believers</u>. They have a submission problem more than a belief problem. The best approach is pray first, speak second.

Verses eighteen through twenty-one has varied Denominational interpretations. It is not this study's intent to generate debate, only suggestion and discussion. Why did Jesus go to preach to dead people from the time of Noah? What would be the point? <u>Certainly suggesting a second chance at Salvation is a stretch</u>. Nowhere does Scripture offer such a plan. If a second chance is plausible, the five complacent virgins in that Parable worried needlessly! <u>Did Christ descend to tell dead people from Abraham to Noah they retroactively have been saved by His resurrection</u>? A case can be made that His victory over the grave is retroactive. Or is Peter referencing cast-out beings from the spiritual realm which the Bible often speaks of? Genesis 6 indicates some did sexually mate with human women. Or do these verses simply proclaim to this place of the dead that God's plan for the ages is completed in Christ's Resurrection? <u>This would support Christ's victory as retroactive for the children of Abraham.</u> For certain, rampant wickedness in Noah's time brought Judgment. Water was both a saving device and Judgment device. Eight emerged from the water and are a New Testament symbol of Deliverance. One final consideration, Peter is reminding readers that just as Christ worked through Noah, Christ works through believers to make Sanctification complete.

Application

Husbands and wives are to govern their lives in relation to one another. This is mandated by Covenant. When a divorce occurs, you can bet that one or both spouses invested their lives to either children, relatives, career or some other diversion.

Submitting to the will of the Father puts you in some good company; first Jesus, then the Apostles. <u>As in the days of Noah, one must submit to the Lord to be saved</u>.

1 PETER 4
Suffering and Sanctification walk Hand-in-Hand

The case is continued, suffering for doing good puts you in the company of Christ. But being in His Company carries responsibilities beginning with; Him being positioned in our life as our first love rather than other interests. (Revelation 2:4)

Read 1 Peter 4:1-11

1) Compare verse one with 1 Peter 3:17-18

2) When a Christian suffers for the Faith, what decision has that person made? (v. 2)

3) Just as a Christian is assured of escaping eternal condemnation, what equally will unbelievers be assured is their fate for having lived apart from God? (v. 5)

Discussion:

Compare verse six with 1 Peter 3:18-20. Consider also Hebrews 9:27; 12:23. Who might these dead people be and why do you think they are referenced? For helpful insight, see **Time-Out** in Helicopter Overview of this lesson.

4) How might verse seven be motivation to live a godly lifestyle?

5) Why is it important not to put-off getting one's lifestyle on track with godly living? (v. 7)

6) What do you say to one who professes Christ but whose life is a reflection of the values of the world? See Matthew 25:13

7) What is one of the significant benefits of love according to verse eight?

8) Regarding verse ten, of what Grace is Peter is speaking? See 1 Corinthians 12:1-11

Read 1 Peter 4:12-19
9) When you suffer, how much thought do you give to Christ?

10) Name a time you were insulted or maligned because of Christ?

11) What does the Bible say concerning Judgment and the Church? (v. 17) See also 2 Corinthians 5:1-10

12) What is the message of verse eighteen? (See note below)

Note: <u>Before answering this question</u>, read Amos 7:7-9, Revelation 20:11-15 and consider that the plumb-line for man's standard is the Ten Commandments.

Discussion:
What do you think it means that believers groan while waiting to join Christ?

Summary Statement:
Whatever the suffering for good works, this suffering is not a useless thing in the eyes of God. To have suffered in the Faith, great reward awaits in Heaven.

As related in the previous chapter, one need not submit to being nailed to a tree to demonstrate a willingness to suffer. In modern society a Christian is not likely to suffer physical abuse for the Gospel. Verses two and three indicate abstention from worldly pleasures is the extent we are called to please God. Some may suffer if they don't drive a luxury car or live in a big home with a swimming pool. But this kind of suffering has nothing to do with the Gospel. <u>It is an ungodly mind who dwells on luxuries they can't afford</u>. The Bible tells us to be content with what God gives us. *"Be content with what you have."* (Hebrews 13:5)

Verse six might appear to be related to 1 Peter 3:19 where some controversy exists. Here we cannot say the dead in verse six is inclusive of the Old Testament dead. There was no Gospel to be heard prior to Christ. <u>Old Testament Saints did exist but for a different reason</u>. *"Abraham believed God, and it was credited to him as righteousness."* (Romans 4:3)

Time Out: Verse six requires <u>understanding Peter's letter is one of encouragement</u>. Reminders of godly living appear but specifically, Peter assures readers that family and friends (Mostly Jewish converts) who died after receiving the Gospel still retain their position in Christ. Knowing this would strengthen their Faith and keep their Sanctification alive until Jesus' return.

Verse seven has a dual message. It is hyperbole to not delay godly living. The Parable of the Ten Virgins (Matthew 25:1-13) is the principle applied here. Second, the Church Age will end at the return of Christ. (Revelation 4:1) After that, it's all about Daniel's seventieth week and the redemption of Israel. (Daniel 9:20-27)

Though difficult in the moment, being maligned because of Christ is a good thing. <u>It says something about you</u>. It is Christ being persecuted, not you! This is not your loss, it is your antagonist. *"For they do not know what they are doing."* (Luke 23:34)

<u>Attacking Christian values has been with us for centuries.</u> Unfortunately in our day, some pundits seem delighted when Christian values are attacked! It offers them opportunity for political and financial gain. These are not Christians but opportunists, who would have us believe persecution is a recent phenomenon that began when their guy doesn't win political office. The truth is, Christians have been under attack since A.D. 33.

Listening to pundit rhetoric disguised as Christian is sickening. These wolves in sheep's clothing lead many into sin by imparting innuendo, suspicion and fear that gives birth to hate into the hearts of naïve souls. <u>A Christian should be building bridges to the lost, not burning them</u>. All men are victims and all men were at one time lost! (1 Peter 4:3) No, not one of us were born saved! (Ecclesiastes 7:20, Romans 3:10) The Apostle Paul himself, was one such persecutor of the early Church.

Certainly the Grace of God in Christ freely given is man's avenue to Salvation. <u>But God gives each of us a second kind of Grace; spiritual gifts.</u> (1 Corinthians 12:4-11) These are the skills God grants His people to serve His family. Foolishly, prideful individuals credit themselves for the skills they possess. A true believer knows this is not the case. They know all gifting comes from above.

<u>Application</u>

"I am the vine, you are the branches. He who abides in me, and I in him, bears much fruit." (John 15:5 NKJV) The message of the opening two verses in this chapter is our application. <u>Refrain from being led into what seems right with the world</u>. This is contingent upon to whom we listen! For as we listen so shall we think. As we think so shall we do! Abiding in the Word and gathering with other believers on a regular basis is paramount to arming our self with the *Armor of God*. (v.1)

Notes for 1 Peter 4

Journal for the Week

A. Relational Victory

B. Relational Challenges

C. Personal Victories

    a. Overcoming hidden sin or sin harmful to a family member or friend.

    b. Bad habit diminished, or good one either started or sustained.

D. Personal Challenges

1 PETER 5
Shepherding

How beautiful are the feet of those who bring good news!" (Romans 10:14-15) The Spirit in which spiritual overseers deliver the Gospel is examined. For them, a Crown of Glory awaits. Respect for elders is also examined.

Read 1 Peter 5:1-11

1) What are all Christians called upon to store-up for themselves? See Matthew 6:20

2) Name of Crown promised to worthy Pastors and leaders bringing the Gospel.

Crown of _____ (v. 4)

3) There are four additional Crowns in heaven, treasures if you will, one can earn while living on earth. <u>How is each Crown representative of the way we live?</u>

   a. **Crown of Incorruption:** Temperate in all things! 1 Corinthians 9:25 NKJV

   b. **Crown of Life:** Withstands earthen temptations! James 1:12 NKJV (Also martyr's crown)

   c. **Crown of Rejoicing:** Joyous anticipation! 1 Thessalonians 2:19

   d. **Crown of Righteousness:** Abiding love, patient until His appearing! 2 Timothy 4:8

   e. Can Crowns be lost? _____ See Revelation 3:11, Matthew 6:1, 2 John 1:8

Self-Examination:

From the list of five Crowns, which Crown might you be awarded in heaven? What Crown would you like to be preparing now to receive?

4) What is Peter's specific message to young people?

5) What does God say about a proud heart? See Proverbs 16:5

Discussion:

Certainly, Christians are to humble themselves before God? Does that include being humble before men? Would being humble before men exhibit weakness?

6) Regarding verse seven, what additional directions does Philippians 4:6 tell us?

7) Write down and memorize verse eight!

8) Verse eight is one of the great warnings in the New Testament. How are believers to protect themselves from Satan? See Ephesians 6:10-18

9) What six things makeup the Armor of God? What seventh thing enables the six?

1.   2.   3.

4.   5.   6.

7.

10) What vital part of us does Jesus warn can become corrupted? See Luke 21:34-36

11) Grace appears in verse ten and throughout Scripture. A believer must know what the word means because it is a staple of Christianity. What is Grace?

Note: if you must write a lot of words to define Grace, then you really don't know.

Read 1 Peter 5:12-13

12) a. What other Apostle has Silas been associated with? See Acts 15:36-40

b. Peter is associated with Mark. What occurred between Paul and Mark?

13) Who does Peter identify along with Mark as sending His greetings? What kind of place are they all located in? See Ephesians 5:25, Revelation 17:1-6, 18:2-3

Summary Statement:

Re-read 1 Peter 1:1 – Pastors throughout the unbelieving world should minister with a servant's heart. Those being ministered to are to be respectful to elders.

Connecting the dots is essential for Bible study. It is how we get a greater grasp of the Word of God. Certainly the Bible has parts but like a chain, each link links back to previous links. This chapter connects to Romans 10:14-15 which itself links back to Isaiah 52:7. This is why the Bible is so believable. Forty authors writing sixty-six books over 1500 years bring the message of separation and reconciliation in Christ.

Proficiency on a musical instrument entails practice. Any professional musician will tell you hit and miss practice just doesn't cut it. Unfortunately, many believers are hit and miss in practicing the things of the Faith. Therefore, their performance is just as disappointing as the athlete or musician whose practice habits are hit and miss.

Discussion: What things must Christians practice so that they are models for the Faith rather than an embarrassment to the Faith?

Heaven is not attainable through works. If you attend a church whose Theology is riddled with requirements in addition to Christ, Run! John 19:30 means what it says; *"It is finished."* Christ met all requirements for Salvation, not just ninety percent. We do not have to do the other ten percent to be saved. If that were so, Christ would be diminished. <u>Grace has been freely given</u>. Would you not love a man who died in your place? Love for the Lord is manifested in our works. That is what Jesus ask of you and me. *"If you love me, you will obey my commandments."* (John 14:15) It is from our works done in the Spirit for which rewards are given. See Romans 12

It is unlikely Babylon [Revelation 17-18] here refers to a specific geographical location. Babylon is Christian slang (Metaphor) for the heathen idolatrous religious society in which Christians are sojourners. (1 Peter 1:1) She in verse thirteen refers to a body of believers. In verse thirteen, *chosen* links back to Chapter 1 verse one. *Elect* is how Peter first began his letter. John Mark is the same Mark who parted ways with Paul and company during Paul's First Missionary Journey. They later reconciled during Paul's house arrest in Rome. Mark is also the author of the Gospel of Mark. Peter's calling Mark *my son* is indicative of an elder shepherding an underling.

Application

"Be self-controlled and alert. Your enemy the devil prowls around like a roaring lion looking for someone to devour." (v. 8) This verse should have our attention as we go about our daily lives?

Notes for 1 Peter 5

Journal for the Week

A. Relational Victory

B. Relational Challenges

C. Personal Victories

    a. Overcoming hidden sin or sin harmful to a family member or friend.

    b. Bad habit diminished, or good one either started or sustained.

D. Personal Challenges

2 PETER 1
The Importance of Knowledge

The central purpose of this Epistle is postponed to Chapter 2; errant influences and the way to identify them.

Some years have passed since Peter's first Epistle. In that Epistle, Peter identified the real thing (The true Gospel) while addressing problems outside the Church. How external suffering and the Gospel of Christ are interrelated. He feels a quick review of the true Gospel is appropriate. Locate and underline in your Bible the key verse. (v. 13a)

Read 2 Peter 1:1-14

1) If a new driver doesn't have knowledge of the mechanics of operating a car and has no knowledge of traffic flow or signage, what are the consequences if he sets out to drive a car?

2) What is missing in people who are led into cult religions such as was the case in the religious debacles at Jonestown and Waco Texas?

3) Jonestown and Waco are extreme examples of people not knowing the true Gospel of Christ. But perhaps more alarming, what dangers do the lesser extreme religious cults pose on those ignorant of the true Gospel?

4) Without use of a secondary source, write the Gospel of Christ the Bible teaches! (Check what you have written with 1 Corinthians 15:3b-4)

5) What causes corruption in the world? (v. 5)

6) The key word in verse five is *add*. The key word in verse eight is *increasing*. In the context of these two words, what must a person be doing once he/she is saved?

Discussion:
What kind of evidence would a court need to prove one is a Christian?

7) What is promised a mature believer? (vv. 10-11)

Read 2 Peter 1:12-21

8) Compare verses thirteen through fifteen with 2 Timothy 4:6-8

9) What does John 21:15-17 say about Peter's calling?

10) What does Peter say about his witness for the Lord? (v. 16)

11) What is the best kind of witness that something is true? (vv. 16-18)

12) What other accounts can Christians draw from to confirm the Gospel? (vv. 19-21)

13) How are Faith and knowledge interrelated?

Summary Statement:

Maturity, fruit if you will, is a product of knowledge! A baby is a wonderful miracle! If eighteen years later, this baby now a teen, still wears a diaper and cries when its milk bottle is late is not so wonderful! Solid food is the result of <u>increasing in the</u> <u>knowledge</u> of God so that we might grow into the likeness of Jesus Christ.

<u>Faith without foundation is foolish. Faith with a wrong foundation is also foolish!</u> Learning sound Doctrinal Faith is wonderful. But like a newborn, without growth, it is subject to wavering, even collapse if maturity fails to develop. Keeping in mind the subject of the next chapter, (Scoffers and false teachers) Peter sets out to remind readers that <u>in Christ, they are given everything they need</u> to maintain their faith. (Verse 3) Peter makes his case for Christian growth. *"Be eager to make your election sure."* (v. 10) Peter is not suggesting that Salvation needs to be earned. He is talking about evidence that a Christian is really a Christian. (See Application)

Discussion Question: What power is a Christian given?

<u>It is imperative to be found guilty if we are charged with being a Christian!</u> The evidence to convict us rests on the three elements of regeneration being present in our character.

1. Knowledge: Mindful of God. Through study, the mind of God is understood.
2. Wisdom: The extent this knowledge is practiced. (This mind is in you)
3. Christ-like: The absence of this quality sabotages the first two. (Hypocrite)

We shouldn't have to rely on forensics to find a person guilty of being a Christian. It should be as simple as being picked out of a lineup as the one who is loving, kind, gentle, serving and given to integrity. From driving on the roads to checking out at the supermarket, Christian actions are on display to believers and unbelievers alike.

Jesus' miracles, teachings and His Divinity are all recorded by those <u>who had firsthand experience with Him</u>. Those who deny the Christ weren't there so their best case against Jesus is to make stuff up or rely on the words of some other writer who wasn't there either. Or worse, pander to Him by calling Him a good teacher; what an insult! <u>One must question the sanity of those who deny the eyewitness accounts of men and women who walked with Jesus and endured what they endured?</u>

Scoffers are without hope; for they love self and the world more than they love the Lord! Unfortunately, scoffers (2 Peter 2:3-4, Jude 18) often are learned individuals who influence wishy-washy believers to question their faith or worse, corrupt their faith as we shall see in Chapter 2.

Application

If you were arrested and put on trial for being a Christian, would there be enough evidence to convict you?

Notes for 2 Peter 1

Journal for the Week

A. Relational Victory

B. Relational Challenges

C. Personal Victories

    a. Overcoming hidden sin or sin harmful to a family member or friend.

    b. Bad habit diminished, or good one either started or sustained.

D. Personal Challenges

2 PETER 2
Springs Without Water

The Gospel: Some deny it, <u>some misrepresent it</u>, some contaminate it and some trample it by identifying with it for gain or surreptitious purposes. Skeptics and scoffers of the Jesus narrative all have this in common, <u>none of them were there</u>! Seemingly however, all are experts! For them, if Jesus did exist, He was not God incarnate but simply a good teacher. <u>These very people who champion evidence, refute the evidence</u>! Go figure. Eyewitnesses to Christ were many! People who were there tell of Him. Why would anyone take the opinion of scoffers over people who walked with Jesus? Sadly, millions have. This chapter prophecies the time in which we now live.

Read 2 Peter 2

1) In your words, what is the Gospel of Jesus Christ?

2) How might the Gospel be misrepresented? (Consider a rabbit's foot or vending machine)

3) How might the Gospel be contaminated by errant church teachings?

4) How might the Gospel be trampled for gain?

Discussion:

How unthinkable do you think it is that Jesus suffered and died, not to cover His sin, but to cover the sins of people who adamantly deny Him or use His name to profit?

5) What fate awaits those who pervert the sacrifice our Lord made, even for them? (vv. 5-7)

6) **See Romans 13:1**

   a. How does God view those who stand against their government? (v. 10)

   b. If government seems to you as unrighteous, might God condone anarchy?

   c. Who is responsible for judging unrighteous leaders? **See Psalm 110:5-6**

Self-Evaluation: Are you more prone to condemn government leaders than to pray for them? They too are victims of the devil's schemes and in need of Salvation.

7) What is the message of Luke 17:1-3a?

8) How much do you think deception plays out in everyday life?

9) What was the first deception recorded? What resulted? See Genesis 3:1-4, 24

10) Using a dictionary, define *apostasy*.

11) What is the mission of the apostate Church? See 2 Timothy 3:1-7

12) Name a time you were deceived. What were the consequences?

13) Name a time you deceived another person. Was your motive to benefit the other person or was it something else?

Discussion:

Might there ever be a time when lying and deception is justified; Consider Rahab? Should there be condemnation for a good lie?

Summary Statement:

Think of the unschooled mind as a computer without antivirus protection. Being unschooled in the Scriptures opens the mind to a multitude of misinformation. Its end purpose is to separate men from God and to make the faithful believer impotent.

The tone here is much the same as Matthew 23. Don't be blind to the enemy within.

"These things I have spoken to you that you should not be made to stumble." (John 16:1 NKJV) Believers must guard against errant teachers spreading a different gospel. Wolves using Christ to leverage their agendas is another danger for believers not grounded well enough in the Word to identify them. And foremost, we must avoid allowing our own personal appetites to be the source of our wisdom.

People will fall for anything. The number and magnitude of cults make that apparent.

The claims of certain TV Evangelists are ridiculous yet the dollars flow in to them. Religious panache, private jets, exorbitant personal real estate holdings, all bring disrepute to the Faith. Secular society isn't fooled here, so why are believers fooled?

To the Gospel itself, three threats exist. First is the scoffer, the intellectual elite. These are the folks who say the Gospel doesn't meet their intellectual standards for scientific fact. *"For the message of the cross is foolishness to those who are perishing."* What these folks overlook is that science is still evolving! So how they come to their conclusions is anybody's guess. It was once believed the earth was flat. Before that, it was believed the sun, moon and stars rotated around the earth. Sadly, baby Christians and college students are the victims of intellectual scoffers. Have you noticed how skeptics are repulsed by the J word and don't even want to hear the name Jesus? See Mark 5:9-17

The second threat to the Gospel is more dangerous than the first. It looks like the real thing! *"You have a reputation of being alive, but you are dead."* (Revelation 3:1) This church has a steeple atop the building, a choir in the loft and a preacher in the pulpit. The windows are stained, its leaders religiously adorned and the worship service exhibits a great deal of pomp and pageantry. Certainly impressive to the average attendee. The proof is in the pudding! (Theology) Are works and church rituals part of Salvation? If so, RUN! Beloved, this is a Theology that does not fully understand Grace! See Ephesians 2:8-9

The third threat is the more difficult to accept because they are some of our own! But if you have the knowledge of God, *you will know them by their fruit.* What we see today from some serving the Gospel is alarming. They appear politically affiliated! Double-minded service makes one vulnerable to being used by the devil. And it draws immature believers into committing unlawful acts against authority.

Nowhere in Scripture do we find God's messengers demeaning a Roman Emperor, a Governor or taking up arms against established civil authority! To do so is an affront to the Sovereignty of God. Every Head of State is <u>God's instrument to serve His purpose to conclude the human story</u>! In short, we can't vote our way out of God's plan for the ages!

Time Out: It is amazing how Christian's are so shocked when biblical values are compromised in society or even in government edicts. Hello! Are we not wanting Christ to return? <u>Christianity was never designed to make a nation pure! It was designed to save sinners</u>!

Application

Understand Genesis 3:13. Many come to deceive you. <u>Therefore, be well-read in the Scriptures and strong in the Spirit</u>. Be knowledgeable of the Fruit of the Spirit. Reject fruit not produced by the Spirit. Guard against having itching ears. Reject political overtones in the pulpit, for such is contrary to the Spirit of Romans 13:1-7. Reject the hypocrisy behind it. Be on guard for intellectuals who have discovered something the rest of us have missed. And most importantly, fully understand Grace, what it is and what it isn't!

Notes for 2 Peter 2

A. Relational Victory

B. Relational Challenges

C. Personal Victories

    a. Overcoming hidden sin or sin harmful to a family member or friend.

    b. Bad habit diminished, or good one either started or sustained.

D. Personal Challenges

2 PETER 3
Let Us Not Forget

In the days of Noah when the world was filled with violent and wicked men, God used water to destroy them and all they had built. The Bible is clear, history will repeat itself with this exception. Fire will be God's instrument of destruction. Peter is reminding the people he loves, of the things they have been taught. A new Heaven and a new earth await God's people. But <u>there are those who will rob you</u> of this <u>if you listen to them</u>! A Christian's greatest threat is within the Christian community. Beth Moore writes, *"Do you see the frightening truth Judas represents? Yes, it is possible to be in intimate gatherings with Christ, hear His teachings, see His power before our very eyes, and be lost. * Living Beyond Yourself-Beth Moore-Copyright 1998 Reprinted by permission of LifeWay Press ISBN 0-6331-9380-1

Read 2 Peter 3:1-9

1) Has there ever been a time you were just really befuddled when it seemed like God was taking His sweet time? Explain:

2) Compare verse nine with Romans 11:25 and Revelation 9:9-11. What is clarified?

Time Out: Hard to imagine, but sometimes God's decisions aren't always about us!

3) What does Scripture say about the Second Coming of Jesus Christ? See Matthew 24:36 and Matthew 25:1-13

4) Though we cannot know why God is slow to act by our timeline, He does tell us His central plan for the Church? Explain Romans 11:25 and Revelation 6:9-11

5) Which is more dangerous to you and your loved ones, the viper you see in the backyard or the one you don't see under the bed? Why

6) What do you think is the greater threat to a person desiring to live by God's standards, the rhetoric of an atheist or one's own ignorance of the Bible?

Read 2 Peter 3:10-18

7) From Isaiah 2:11-12, do you think the Day of the Lord has to do with Jesus coming for His sheep, or is this about Him coming to defeat His enemies?

8) How does Peter describe the Second Coming of Christ? (v. 10)

9) Some have called 1 Thessalonians 4:13-17 and 2 Peter 3:10 a contradiction. The two have a very different context. Explain the difference.

10) a. Would you welcome the occurrence of the event described in 1 Thessalonians 4:13-17 or do you have unfinished business remaining and are not ready for the Lord to take you to be with Him just yet?

   b. What is the message of Matthew 8:21-22?

Self-Evaluation: If you indicated you have unfinished business and really are not ready for the Lord to take you, what must you do to become ready?

<u>When Jesus comes for you, what of the following things might he find you doing?</u>

In Church - Cutting off another driver - Encouraging someone - Reading the Bible

Making a store clerk laugh - Complaining - Falsifying an insurance claim – Drunk

Writing a check to charity – Spending money you don't have - Praying – Gossiping

Dialed in to an agitator – Cutting in line – Giving-up a place in line – Visiting parents

Telling a lie – Smiling – Singing a hymn – Thinking of another – Being your selfish self

11) Distortion of the Word is not new. Explain the misrepresentation of Scripture Paul is addressing in Romans 6:15-16.

Discussion:
Name instances Christians commit sin, even horrendous evil in the name of God.

Summary Statement:
"Do not be carried away by the error of lawless men." But grow in the grace and knowledge of our Lord and Savior Jesus Christ." (vv. 17-18 paraphrased)

There is an old saying, if someone says something loud enough and often enough, true or not, people will come to believe it! Joseph Goebbels, master propagandist for the Nazis, did exactly this in regard to discrediting the Jews. His efforts led many a good German into being a party to murder. <u>By listening to the message of lawless men and not the Word of God</u>, the biblically ignorant of today are not equipped to discern evil propaganda when they hear it! Result, <u>many will be robbed of their future</u> in the coming Kingdom.

Like Goebbels, lawless men of our generation vilify whomever they please, say whatever they please and worse, people ignorant of the Bible are going to be robbed of their future. About these degraders of others the Lord Jesus said:

"You belong to your father the devil, and you want to carry out your father's desire. He was a murderer from the beginning, not holding to the truth, for there is no truth in him. When he lies, he speaks his native language, for he is a liar and the father of lies." (John 8:44)

Time Out: Growing up even in America, some of us remember hearing adult family members blame the Jews for the country's ills. Today, amnesia is the miracle drug that enables deceivers to lay the country's problems they helped create at someone else's door step.

The lawless men Peter warns of are not anti-god humanist outside the Church. They are apostates and heretics within the Church masquerading as Christians. (Matthew 13:24-30) Raised and educated a Roman Catholic, Joseph Goebbels was amidst a church congregation. Beloved, <u>it is not where you see them, but what you see them doing</u> that gives evidence if their election is of God.

Wholesome living starts with knowing your Bible (vv. 1-2) and ends with doing your Bible. Author Warren Wiersbe writes, "Whoever robs you of God's Word, robs you of your future." Jesus is coming a second time! (v. 10) This is in the Bible! As in the time of Noah, Judgment is again coming upon earth! Peter's call to be spotless (v. 14) is a reminder to the brethren he loves, to <u>mature beyond</u> the things they were taught. Being totally committed to Christ is to be blameless and puts one at peace with God. To follow a false brother into sin or listen to a heretic who places doubt as to Christ's return, robs you of coming face to face with the Savior.

Application

Become what you ought to be as if time is short! Indeed, time is short for the lost! See Ecclesiastes 12:6 The better we know the Word, (v. 2) the better we are equipped to do the work the Lord asks of His people. See Matthew 28:18-2

Notes for 2 Peter 3

Journal for the Week

A. Relational Victory

B. Relational Challenges

C. Personal Victories

    a. Overcoming hidden sin or sin harmful to a family member or a friend.

    b. Bad Habit diminished, good one either started or sustained.

D. Personal Challenges

1 JOHN 1
Eye Witnesses to Our God Revealed

After Adam's fall, could the lost relationship between God and man be restored? For centuries that <u>restoration would remain a mystery until the time when God would come to earth</u> in the Second Person of the Holy Trinity, Jesus. Man was now witness to God in human form.

Irrespective of age, God perceives you as His child if you are identified with this Jesus. This identification is the result of regeneration, born again if you will. In Jesus, you have the right of passage from being a child of Adam to being a child of God. Child is symbolic that there exists a Father that loves and protects. <u>Biblically, protection is being sealed from Satan/spiritual death.</u>

Read 1 John 1-4

1) The first word in John's letter is *"That."* With the aid of the introduction, explain the context of John's use of this word.

2) What four ways were people of Jesus' day able to discern who He was?

3) a. How many times does *we* appear in this section? _____ (vv. 1-5)

   b. Who might be the people John is referring to when he says *we?*

Discussion:
Why do you think John used *we* instead of I?

4) What three things is John offering to His readers?

   1.

   2.

   3.

5) What does John say would make him and those he is associated with joyful?

Read 1 John 1:5-10

6) Sum up the message of verse five.

Discussion:

What are some ways a person who claims Christ still remains in darkness? (v. 6)

7) What do you think Jesus was talking about in the Parable, *a tree and its fruit*? See Matthew 7:15-23

8) From the list, what is the better evidence by which one can identify a Christian?

   a. Sings in the church choir.   b. Carries a Bible to church every Sunday.

   c. Belongs to a specific Denomination.   d. Micah 6:8

   e. Goes to a big church.   f. Goes to a small church.

Time Out: Gnostics and legalists were of serious concern in the early Church. Neither were Christ-centered. Legalist errantly believed Heaven is partially earned by living a set of church established rules and rituals sprinkled in with belief. Gnosticism centered on mysticism in various forms. For both Gnostics and Legalists, Christ's suffering has less meaning than for those who stand on Christ alone! Jesus made it clear at the Cross; *"It is finished."* (John 19:30)

9) Define Grace? In your definition please include the word, Mercy!

Summary Statement:

Knowing who Jesus is and what Jesus has to offer. Secondly, <u>knowing our true self</u> so we are not hypocritical when we align our self with Christ.

The Apostle Paul rightfully is a giant witness for the Gospel. But consider <u>John's hands-on witness</u>! He was with Jesus, witnessing the miracles throughout Jesus' ministry. He observed Jesus' love for others and that the teachings of Jesus were unlike anything John had ever heard. John was present at both the Transfiguration of Jesus and His Ascension. He sat next to Jesus at the Last Supper. He was separated from Jesus and later reunited with the Savior following the Resurrection. It is no wonder His Gospel account of Jesus is the Crown Jewel of the Four Gospels. Matthew wrote of Jesus as having come to Israel as <u>Messiah</u>. Mark portrays Jesus as a <u>Servant</u>, Luke portrays Jesus as a <u>Man</u> and John's Gospel identifies Jesus as <u>God</u>. Jesus is the Revelation of how God would reconcile with human kind.

That refers to a Mystery Revealed! <u>How God would reestablish the broken relationship between Himself and man</u>? John experienced four things that made Jesus believable to him and to us; hearing His words, witnessing His miracles, being with Him and touching Him after the Resurrection. And so it is with us, we have to hear His words before we can see Him and be touched by Him.

So why should anyone believe John or other witnesses of Jesus? Some say because we are to believe by faith and though that is true, there is something very tangible worth mentioning. Would John and others such as Paul devote an entire life, endure persecution, even die for a lie? Would not at some point they became weary if the Jesus story was a sham? It is because of these men and women who are forever etched on the pages of history, our Bibles, we too are caught up!

The chapter's final point is this. Anyone who says they are incapable of sin because they live in the Spirit are themselves deceived. Not even the Apostle Paul could do that. (Romans 7:18-19, 2 Corinthians 12:9) Scripture never ever says the flesh can become sinless. The best of Christians do sin as John states. Which is exactly why we need Christ as our Savior.

Application

First, be thankful for this verse; *"It is finished!"* (John 19:30) Second, I will live my life as outlined in Romans 12:1. *"Therefore, I urge you, brothers, in view of God's mercy, to offer your bodies as living sacrifices, holy and pleasing to God – this is your spiritual act of worship."*

Notes for 1 John 1

Journal for the Week

A. Relational Victory

B. Relational Challenges

C. Personal Victories

    a. Overcoming hidden sin or sin harmful to a family member or a friend.

    b. Bad habit diminished, good one either started or sustained.

D. Personal Challenges

1 JOHN 2
What Should or Shouldn't Your Passion Be?

How great the Father's love for us that we should be called children of God. Even more, when we stumble, our heavenly Father has made a way to forgive us. Our part is to keep a heart of thankfulness. We demonstrate this by doing His Commandments starting with the First Commandment? This is obligatory for a Christian. For one cannot love the Lord while holding to a life that resembles the world.

Read 1 John 2:1-14

1) When a person stands accused in a court of law, who defends the accused?

2) From Revelation 20:11-12, what is going to take place one day?

3) Who stands a better chance for a better outcome in a trial, the man who defends himself or a man who depends upon a competent advocate?

4) Who is your accuser before God and why is Christ better qualified to defend you than you defending yourself? See Revelation 12:10 and Hebrews 4:14-16

5) Who enables God's people to be obedient to God's commands? See Romans 5:5

6) What are the three stages of maturity every Christian goes through? (vv. 12-14)

Read 1 John 2:15-17

7) What does John say happens to a Christian whose passion is to love the world?

8) From the following list, rank in order from first to last your passion at this age.

	Age 18-30	Age 30-60	Age 60 +
Family & Friends	_____	_____	_____
Career	_____	_____	_____
Growing in the Lord	_____	_____	_____
Acquiring more/experiencing more	_____	_____	_____
Other	_____	_____	_____

Personal Thought: What do you learn about yourself and do you like what you see?

Read 1 John 2:18-29

9) Why do you think Satan would rather deceive God's children than unbelievers?

10) What are some of the dangers of complacent Christian living?

Discussion:

What does it mean to be *with us* but not *of us*?

11) How important is it, and what are the benefits, for Christians to assemble on a regular basis?

Discussion:

Why might a Christian think they have a license to sin? Do you think it is possible that a person thinks they are saved when in reality, they are not?

12) For certain, one who denies Jesus is lost. But what is John's emphatic emphasis in verse twenty-four?

13) a. What are some ways Christians can be led into errant beliefs concerning Heaven and hell?

    b. What are some ways that even one's own church might diminish its members' passion for the Lord? See Revelation 3:14-18

14) Write down and memorize this passage of Scripture. Galatians 5:22

Summary Statement:

Jesus suffered death, even unto being nailed to a tree to save us. Do not be deceived, we cannot say we know Him while living a life that contradicts our claim. The Christian Faith is a lifetime of growing. The world's pleasures can overcome anyone who ceases to abide in Jesus. Do not be complacent, for we are in the last days.

A Father's love includes concern for how His children live. This chapter is a hands-on dialogue of a father raising up godly children. First and foremost, making them wise to the Word of God and what they have been given in Christ. Warnings that are issued include, how the world and the love of it offers nothing of permanence. To be alert to the deceptions of men who themselves, are misguided and offer nothing of value. The words of such men are designed by the enemy to separate us from the Father.

First, let's clear up verse eighteen as to the meaning of the word *hour*. Here, John is referring to the spirit of antichrist being in the world. This not to be confused with the *time of the Gentiles*. For that is a different subject on which passages from the Book of Daniel addresses. (Daniel 2:31-45, 7:1-27, 8:1-26)

John simply uses the term *hour* to give a sense of urgency. A sense of staying alert to the influences around us every day. God's people should guard against drifting into complacency! John exhorts his readers to live a life they would not be ashamed to be engaged in when Christ returns for them. (1 Thessalonians 4:16-17)

Living God's way John writes, is for us to recognize that we are part of an eternal family. We are to love this family and be active in the edification of one another.

God's family has enemies and they are active enemies. Therefore, naivety is to be avoided. John warns believers not to get caught up in worldly living. We call them today carnal Christians. They are believers whose living resembles much that of unbelievers. The blessing of a close relationship with the Savior is diminished if not entirely lost when engaging worldly living! Living in the Spirit spares us the danger of a separation from God. Separation from God is undeniably, the enemy's goal.

Application

God loves you so much that He gave His Son for you. What a wonderful hope! How important is the Father's love to you? Surely it is important enough to correct those things in our character that grieves the Spirit. Joyce Meyer has a wonderful book, 'The Battle Field of the Mind' that is worth your time.

Notes for 1 John 2

Journal for the Week

A. Relational Victory

B. Relational Challenges

C. Personal Victories

    a. Overcoming hidden sin or sin harmful to a family member or a friend.

    b. Bad habit diminished, good one either started or sustained.

D. Personal Challenges

1 JOHN 3
A New Identity

A Christian does not suffer an identity crisis! This is one of the most substantive chapters in all Scripture pertaining to what it means to be one of God's children. In short, <u>to be a child of God is by the Mercy of God</u>. In Christ, we are given this right of passage to Eternal Kingdom Living. To whom do you belong?

Read 1 John 3:1-10

1) Who are the children of God? See John 1:11-12; Romans 9:6-8

Discussion:

Perhaps election should be included as part of this lesson. Read Romans 9:9-18 and access the compatibility of election and mercy

2) Compare 1 John 3:2-3 with John 1:11-12 and Jesus' conversation with Nicodemus in John 3:3-8. Explain how you as a believer will be like Jesus.

3) *"We shall be like Him, for we shall see Him as He is."* (v. 2) It is important a Christian understand three essentials terms of the Faith. Using a Bible dictionary, define the following.

   a. Sanctified

   b. Justified

   c. Glorified

4) Name some things that damage relationships with:

   a. Family

   b. Friends

   c. God

Read 1 John 3:11-24

5) Name things that are obligatory to having a good relationship with:

    a. Family

    b. Friends

    c. God

6) In spite of your best efforts, there is strife between you and another person. What directions does the Apostle Paul relate to this situation? See Romans 12:17-18

7) Polar opposites are two hearts, the cold heart and the oversensitive heart. (vv. 19-23)

    a. Describe the cold hearted person.

    b. How does verse twenty offer relief to the oversensitive heart?

8) Do you think it is possible to live by correct doctrines, go to church, read the Bible, sing in the church choir and still grieve the Spirit by a lack of love? What does Scripture say about this type of individual? See 1 Corinthians 13:1

9) Look up the word *abide* in your dictionary and relate this meaning to Jesus.

10) Explain the difference between Salvation and fruit bearing.

Summary Statement:

"Now we are the children of God." (v. 2) The Christian life is not compatible with habitual sin.

A Father's words of love to His children continues unfolding beautifully in this chapter. How important it is to recognize God as our Father. The Bible tells us the way to recognize and accept Him as our Eternal Father is through the Son. <u>Have you done that</u>? If you haven't, do so before you leave this earth!

Let's be clear, not all people are God's children. Think of your own children who are born from your seed. Then consider the other children in your neighborhood. <u>It is your own you give the right of inheritance</u>! Yes, God loves all of His Creation, but not all of His creatures does He grant the right of inheritance! Only those, like Isaac, who are born of the Spirit (Regenerated) has a birthright inheritance! To be fully correct with your answer to the second question, *born of the Spirit* must appear.

It should be pointed out that being a child of God does not make one incapable of committing sin as some believe. <u>No one is ever cured, only washed</u>. All dirty themselves, but God's children we are not disinherited because of dirt. Failures grieve the Spirit certainly, but God's promise is unshakable: *"I am with you always"* Even in failure, Jesus washes you white as snow. Christ died to commute past, present and future sins of God's Elect. Now habitual sin is another matter and John addresses this in verse six. John reinforces the words Jesus spoke in Matthew 7:15-16. *"You will know them by their fruit."*

Even in the magnificence of God's love, warnings appear in this chapter. First, for those who lead others astray and second, to guard the love in our hearts. Paul writes in 1 Corinthians of possessing noble things. But then Paul writes, if love is absent, such a gifted person is but a resounding gong or a clanging cymbal.

The essence of the message of Christ John identifies in verse eleven. *To love one another!* Not to love is paramount to murder John writes. <u>Not to love carries with it the same penalty as physical murder</u>. (v.15) In essence, love is tantamount to escaping the fires of everlasting torment. For God descended in the person of Jesus for one reason, love. Those who, demean, denigrate and hate we surmise would kill some people were it not for laws against murder. Malice is in their heart and God sees it!

The Christian life is not compatible with hate or habitual sin. In the economy of God, habitual sin includes ongoing selfishness, narcissism, and self-sufficiency.

Application

Question: How should a Christian be living in this world? Write down verse twenty-three.

Notes for 1 John 3

Journal for the Week

A. Relational Victory

B. Relational Challenges

C. Personal Victories

    a. Overcoming hidden sin or sin harmful to a family member or a friend.

    b. Bad habit diminished, good one either started or sustained.

D. Personal Challenges

1 JOHN 4
The Child of God is Defined by Wisdom and Love

As writers of the New Testament often do, they address the subject of false teachers. This would include pseudo-Christian wolves who have hidden themselves amongst the flock. As we have said in previous chapters, these are far more dangerous than those who are upfront in their opposition to the Faith.

The core subject of this chapter is love. Love is the means by which one's son-ship is tested. Love limited to reading of it in the Bible or reciting Bible verses about love is nothing more than plugging in a lamp. Not until the lamp is turned on will its light shine! John cautions believers to discern the lamps of others. If they shine a light that is pure, they are of God. If their light emits a party-ball glow of various colors, beware!

Read 1 John 4:1-6

1) The face and methods of false religious teaching has changed but its source remains unchanged. Who is the source of false church teachings?

2) What are the dangers of false teaching in regard to Salvation?

Discussion:

What are just some of the errant viewpoints in the world today about the way of Salvation and the person of Jesus? What is Pluralism? Who do you think is more difficult to witness to, an Atheist or one who believes in Pluralism and why?

3) Describe the difference in your conversation patterns when you are among believers and unbelievers.

4) Describe the relationship of verse three with 2 Thessalonians 2:1-4 and the Second Coming of our Lord. See also Revelation 6:2 and Revelation 19:11

Discussion:

2 Thessalonians 2:4 describes antichrist positioning himself in God's Temple. Does that mean the Temple in Jerusalem will be rebuilt? Given today's political climate, this seems unlikely. Or perhaps the Temple refers to the hearts of men or perhaps the Church itself. What do you think?

Read 1 John 4:7-21

5) Do you believe love is best demonstrated by an emotional feeling or action?

6) How was God's love made manifest in the world? (vv.9-10)

7) Because of what God did in the person of Jesus, what are you to do?

8) What is the best way to identify a person indwelled by the Holy Spirit?

9) What do you say of the person who correctly identifies who Jesus is?

10) What way can you be like Jesus and fear nothing when Judgment comes? (v. 21)

11) What contradicts the claims of anyone who says he is a born again Christian when it would seem he is not? (v. 8, 20)

Self-Examination:

How broad is your love of others? Are you one who practices exclusivity? Do you delight in keeping secrets with some family members that shut another family member out? Is your circle of those you actively love small, medium, large? What position does Christ have in your life? See Revelation 2:4

Discussion:

Explain some ways how self-deception of one's own Christianity is accomplished by the devil.

12) From this chapter, was it man who first reached out to God or did God make the first move toward reconciliation? (v. 10)

Summary Statement:

"Dear friends, let us love one another, for love comes from God." (v. 7)

John takes up the subject of false teaching. Scripture presents a fervent case to oppose apostasy. But beloved, some in the Faith have gone completely off the rails by viewing elected officials and government as the enemy. This takes the focus off the real enemy. It is the devil who triumphs when this happens. Because, when the doors of suspicion and fear of officials are opened, sin comes right on in and makes itself comfortable. Rome, the Emperor or the local Governor were never the focus of derision of Paul, John or even Jesus. It is, and has always been, the apostate church that sends millions to ruin, not government! So please, can the Church not continue as a political pawn of the devil, so that the real enemy can be identified?

Since John's day, false teaching has evolved to include numerous individuals who claimed revelation from God. These men/and women wrote their own religious book apart from the forty writers of the Bible. After which, their first followers declared it a religion. There was no sacrifice, no miracles or any witness of a divine deity. <u>These misguided souls were, like all followers of deception, sincere in what they believed!</u> Today, the world is awash in false religions, karmas and pluralism that appear like the real thing. Some have a choir, a pulpit, stained glass windows, mahogany pews and a building with a steeple. And in come the deceived by the thousands, marching to their destruction. Oh yes, the founder himself, he never performed any miracle or has he/she left the grave they were put in!

Until a pumpkin has all its inner gunk removed and holes opened for eyes and a mouth, it will never be useful to light a darkened area. Love for one another is evidence the Spirit of God is living inside. The followers of Jesus are wired to love others. So it follows, love for other believers is obligatory. <u>Not to gather on a regular basis with our heavenly family is certain to breed a rusty kind of love.</u>

Application

Love begins with loving the Lord. All other love follows after this Commandment.

"Love the Lord your God with all your heart and with all your soul and with all your mind." (Matthew 22:37) <u>Love was never meant to be small!</u> *"For God so loved the <u>whole world</u> that He gave His only begotten Son."* (John 3:16) The test of our Christianity is not inside our special little circle. Beloved, it is out there, over yonder, even that person you have rejected! Do you see?

Notes for 1 John 4

Journal for the Week

A. Relational Victory

B. Relational Challenges

C. Personal Victories

    a. Overcoming hidden sin or sin harmful to a family member or a friend.

    b. Bad habit diminished, good one either started or sustained.

D. Personal Challenges

1 JOHN 5
Love for God Identified

Habitual sin must first be recognized before it can be addressed then avoided. If you are one who consciously obeys your heavenly Father's commands, you are blessed in that, you demonstrate love for the Lord and are assured His love is in you! Hallelujah! This manner of love is not burdensome. (v. 3) Loving the Father is exhibited when one loves the Son. The fruit of this love is the <u>avoidance of habitual sin</u>. (v. 4)

Read 1 John 5:1-12

1) What might it feel like to be at peace with God? What things come into play?

2) To be at peace with God, what first must all men do?

3) What do you think it means to be at war with God? Where does this war start?

4) What is the difference between occasional sinful slips and habitual sin?

5) What does Ephesians 2:2 say about the children of disobedience?

6) Even though the believer has acquired the Divine Seed, there is still the old nature (flesh) present. When you stumble, name two things you should do! See 1 John 1:9 and Isaiah 55:7

Read 1 John 5:13-21

7) What confidence do believers have when they turn to the Lord?

Discussion:

Verse sixteen is a long verse and may be difficult to understand what kind of death John alludes to here, physical or spiritual death. John actually says there are people for which prayer is not suggested. (v. 16) What might be John's message here? See *Notes for 1 John 5* for insight to this issue at the end of this lesson.

8) Using a Bible Dictionary, look up Gnostics and draw a parallel of these people that existed in John's time to a similar mind-set of people in the present time.

9) John explains that Satan has control of the whole world. This being true, what must a person do to not suffer Judgment when it comes?

10) John's final warning to his readers concerns idols. How do idols damage one's relationship with the Lord?

11) How are the idols of today different from John's day?

12) What ought the believer to have in his/her mind when going to God? (v. 14)

13) Which of these selections least threatens the Faith?

    a. Idols   b. Government   c. False doctrines.

Explain your reasoning:

Summary Statement:

The legitimacy of being in Christ calls for the Christian life to be free of habitual sin.

Uncle Chuck hid two Easter eggs and challenged his young niece and nephew to a contest to see who could find the two eggs first. On his command to start, neither child moved. Instead, the brother and sister joined hands and began looking for the two eggs together. When asked why they didn't compete, the older brother replied; "If one of us found both eggs, that would leave the other one sad."

The values of this material world is in marked contrast to this story. And this can make habitual sin difficult to recognize. Because getting the upper hand *is* the principle value of this world. Besting another person just seems so normal. Even personal behavior; crude talk, cursing, gossiping, running others down, when practiced long enough, the mere repetition of it, makes it seem perfectly normal.

There are Christians who only perceive sin as being sexual, law-breaking or committing violence. So if they are not engaged in such acts, they do not see themselves as sinning. For some, even violence is biblically justified.

There are cases of people who haven't picked up a phone to call an aging parent for decades. But because they teach a children's Sunday school others consider them godly people.

With deception so very normal in some professions, those so engaged see nothing wrong with it. It is appalling what is compromised in the political arena or the advertising industry. Ambiguity, fabrication, half-truths, innuendo, character assassination to downright lying are tools of the trade. Rare do we hear a political supporter limit talk to the virtues of their candidate. To the contrary, given a microphone, they invariably engage in the aforementioned activities; blatant sin! Even some Christian advocates suggest in politics, God gives a free pass! Really?

In his book, "The Road to Character," David Brooks identifies two kinds of people; Adam One and Adam Two. Adam One finds reward in defeating others. We see this all the time in traffic. On the other hand, Adam Two is rewarded simply by serving others. This suggests that <u>the habitual sinner needs a change in what he values.</u> Brooks identifies the late George C. Marshal as an Adam Two type who, like Jesus, saw more value in serving others rather than besting them for his own gain.

It is an oxymoron, an illusion, a lie if you will, when a person says they love the Lord but live in habitual sin. Satan has deluded their minds to the point they are comfortable trampling the law of love. Verse three recites that God's commands are not burdensome. <u>For the person who finds God's commands burdensome, it is time to change the things that are loved</u>! Verse eighteen is a wakeup call to perhaps even changing jobs, changing friends or activities. Perhaps they should learn <u>to admire a different kind of person</u>. Certainly John is not speaking of advertising jobs or politics here but the principles of which he speaks do not change to accommodate the circumstances.

All this said, the central issue of this chapter is Christ; His legitimacy, His Spirit and His sacrifice. His water baptism represents the new birth of Jesus the man. His blood represents His sacrifice and the Spirit is the Father's acknowledgment of the two.

Application

Write down and memorize Romans 8:37-38

Notes for 1 John 5

Verse sixteen is interpreted differently by Christians because we read of the power of prayer in the Bible. And prayer *is* powerful for the child of God! It puts the person in communion with God. But what John is saying here is, prayer is a precious and holy thing so don't waste it. <u>Avoid praying for good things to come the way of those who reject God or believe He doesn't even exist</u>? Jesus said much the same thing when He said; "Do not give what is holy to dogs, nor cast your pearls before swine." (Matthew 7:6)

Christians praying for good fortune to come to an unbeliever, loved one or otherwise, to get a good job or to get a promotion is useless. God doesn't hear such prayers. Numerous Psalms and Proverbs tell of God turning a deaf ear to even His Covenant People when they are rebellious to Him. Certainly unbelief is rebellion! So it stands to reason, God is not in the business of granting prayers benefiting unbelievers. The only prayer we should offer on behalf of an unbelieving loved one is for their Salvation.

Accessing the Scriptures

2 & 3 JOHN
Christian Health

<u>A healthy church is not determined by the preacher</u> or a debt free building. It is determined by its Doctrine and its people. In these two brief letters, John identifies characteristics of a healthy body of believers. They are neither hypocritical, weak, or do they fabricate denominational gunk not directed by Scripture. (v.9) Such practices invite exclusivism. John 3 cites an example whereby association with some religious types simply are to be avoided.

Read John 2

1) Why go to a church anyway? Why is it necessary to gather with other believers?

2) The Church has its critics and some of the criticism is valid. That said, <u>those who criticize the Church most likely still wouldn't attend if the Church were perfect</u>. But imagine a nation without visible churches; none, zilch! How do none attenders and the society itself benefit from the thousands of Churches they never attend?

3) What does a church with stained glass windows, active music department, many programs, catchy web site and close proximity to home tell you about the church?

4) Certainly Christians are not to judge people. It is up to God to do that. But John does call upon Christians to be neither naive nor ignorant. Verse four identifies some who walk in truth which is a clear indication <u>some must not walk in truth</u>. Assuming one's belief is not in question, how then is truth in them exhibited?

5) What is the primary tool of one who is controlled by the spirit of antichrist? (v.7)

6) a. What rules in an atmosphere of extreme fundamentalism?

   b. What is missing when extreme fundamentalism is practiced?

Discussion:

The Gospels in no way describe Jesus as an extreme fundamentalist. In fact, living with Jesus is easier than living with a fundamentalist! Why might some believers insist on extreme fundamentalism in guiding family, themselves and their church?

Read 3 John

7) What are some of the wrong reasons to select a church home?

8) As believers, all of us at one time have visited a church for the first time. If it happened to be a day Communion was observed, were all believers invited to the table or was it only available for members of that Denomination? How did you feel when you as a believer, was not allowed at the Lord's Table?

   a. Would you say such a church is Christ centered or church centered?

   b. What are the dangers of a congregation that is church centered?

   c. Why or why not would you seek membership in this church?

   d. What law of Christ is being violated when a church excludes visiting believers from the Lord's Table?

9) According to John, the Church should be sustained by believers only. (v. 7) What does it say about Evangelists, TV or otherwise, who solicit for, and accept financial support from anyone, believers or nonbelievers, willing to write a check?

Discussion:

Do you think a political party should try to identify with Christ? What might be the motive? What do the responsibilities of identifying with Christ carry? If Christ is claimed by a political party, does that indicate that one must be a member of that political party to be saved?

10) John describes a strong-willed leader in a church who loved the limelight and dismissed outsiders. How might this situation become entrenched in a church?

Summary Statement:

Love your brothers and sisters in Christ. Exclusiveness has no place in the Faith. Elitism is worldly and, along with false doctrines, are to be purged from the Church.

<u>A church can bring you down as well as lift you up</u>. Revelation 2 & 3 testifies to this truth. We are in error to select a church because of its elaborate structure, vast facilities, infinite programs, music extravaganzas or a preacher who is a polished orator. This is not to say churches with these things are bad churches. This is to say, love for the Lord is the soul of a church. After that, all these things are simply a bonus.

A church loaded with denominational gunk offers nothing and is even dangerous to attend. If a church seems too religious it probably is. Why, because it is not Christ centered. It is imperative to know the difference between a Christ centered church and one that is church centered. <u>Christ saves, not the institutional church!</u> The institutional church is simply the tool for the Body to assemble. If you find a Body of caring believers whose doors are open to all and who live, love, breathe and teach Christ, join it!

The lady addressed in John 2 could be a woman who perhaps meets a church in her home. But most likely, lady here refers simply to the Institutional Church and children refers to the membership. Lady is indicative of the Church being the Bride of Christ. (Ephesians 5:22-29) In these two short letters, John expresses love and encouragement to two church leaders. We observe that he is pleased with those who exhibit love for one another. We also get the feeling two ill winds are blowing; religious aristocracy (Exclusiveness) and false teaching. (Apostasy) Let's be clear, religious exclusiveness is alive and well in the doctrines of many denominational gatherings today. Nowhere in the Gospel accounts did Jesus construct an aristocracy.

One classic example that Jesus is available to all who receive Him is the woman at the well. (John 4:7-26) <u>Still, churches often engage in disenfranchising many</u>.

A canvas of Doctrines today reveals a laundry list of denominational gunk. Were the founding Apostles alive today, they undoubtedly would just about have a stroke with the bridges being burned and what's being required for Salvation.

John's direction here sets a criteria for a healthy church. It begins with the leaders in the body of Christ possessing a servant's heart and demonstrating a <u>love for the flock that is effective to the *whole* membership</u>.

Application

"Keep me from deceitful ways; be gracious to me through your law.
I have chosen the way of truth; I have set my heart on your laws.
I hold fast to your statutes, O Lord: do not let me be put to shame.
I run in the path of your commands, for you have set my heart free."

Psalm 119:29-32

Notes for John 2 & 3

Journal for the Week

A. Relational Victory

B. Relational Challenges

C. Personal Victories

    a. Overcoming hidden sin or sin harmful to a family member or a friend.

    b. Bad Habit diminished, good one either started or sustained.

D. Personal Challenges

JUDE
Grace is not a License to Sin

"What shall we say, then? Shall we go on sinning so that grace may increase?
By no means! We died to sin; how can we live in it any longer?"

Romans 6:1-2

Jude could have ended the Bible with Faith, Jesus, love or some other subject. But he is compelled by the Holy Spirit to provide the Bible's <u>final warning regarding sin</u>.

Jesus did not die so as to grant a free pass to sin! Jude's letter is a call to be solidly grounded in the Word so that deception will not play a role in our lives such as it did with Eve. An ungrounded believer is easy prey for the devil's agents.

Read Jude 1-16

1) Jude was eager to write to his friends about the Faith. But what circumstances changed the subject he would write about?

2) a. From verse four, where will we surprisingly find people that could be a danger to a believer's walk of Faith?

   b. Who are these sly foxes and why do they pose a danger, especially to new believers? See 2 Timothy 3:5-6

3) What fate awaited angels and men who compromise responsibility to the Lord?

4) What are some of the responsibilities of a Christian?

Discussion:

Why do you think Jude reminds his readers of things they already know?

5) What sin do you think people are exercising when they reject authority? See Romans 13:1-2, Proverbs 16:18

Discussion:

We are probably unaware that people slander heaven's beings. What are ways that one might slander angels and not be aware of doing it? (vv. 8-10)

6) Jude refers to men living by their instincts as perishing by those instincts. (v. 10) How does a believer's way of living differ from an animal?

7) a. What is the way of Cain? See Genesis 4:3-7

   b. Who was Balaam and what was his error? Deuteronomy 23:3-6

   c. Who was Korah and what was his rebellion? See Numbers 16:1-3, 28-33

8) Why might it be dangerous for a Christian to consort with the crowd that continually takes a rebellious attitude towards government and elected officials?

9) In all probability, who are the holy ones prophesied by Enoch in verse fourteen? See 1 Thessalonians 4:16-17, Revelation 19:11-14

10) Read Revelation 6:11, 7:9, Revelation 3:4-6 and explain as if explaining to an unbeliever, the significance of Scripture's use of the term *white robe.*

Read Jude vv. 17-25

11) From verse nineteen, why do some people live a carnal life while others honor God by how they live?

12) What does it mean to pray in the Spirit? See Romans 8:26-27, Galatians 4:6

Discussion:

What are Christians responsible to do according to verses twenty-two and twenty-three?

13) Whose strength will you rely on to do the things God asks of you? (v. 24)

Summary Statement:

The words to the hymn, "Jesus paid it All," is not meant as a license to sin.

Satan loves an undressed Christian because he can make them appear as a hypocrite! Christian standards are of no value if in not recognizing sin, people with ungodly agendas draw us in. In the early days of teller training, tellers worked with genuine currency. Surprisingly, tellers were never introduced to counterfeit currency. One would think training would involve handling phony money. But the theory was, if the teller is only exposed to the real thing, they will quickly recognize a counterfeit.

To put Jude into today's perspective, the Christian community is quick to contend against external attacks on the Faith but seemingly oblivious to internal dangers. These are those individuals of influence who quickly identify with Jesus but in reality, their father is the devil. (John 8:44) They use the Faith not to win the lost, but to worm their way into people's minds via media venues. Some even occupy pulpits. (1 Timothy 3:5-6) Jude is not talking about individuals teaching a false gospel; modern imposters are too foxy to ever do that! What these self-styled Christians do and do so well is divide people against one another. Their weapon of choice is suspicion, innuendo and fear. Government leaders are their usual suspect. How quickly people forget they are challenging God's Sovereignty. Defiance of authority doomed certain angels and men such as Korah and his followers. (Numbers 16:1-33) *"These are the men who divide you, who follow mere natural instincts and do not have the Spirit."* (v. 19)

Paul takes the same stance as does Jude. *"For such men are false apostles, deceitful workmen, masquerading as apostles of Christ. And no wonder for Satan himself masquerades as an angel of light. It is not surprising then, if his servants masquerade as servants of righteousness."* (2 Corinthians 11:13-15)

Verses twenty-two to the end is the Bible's final words about being more than a convert.

Application
"Build yourselves up in your most holy faith and pray in the Holy Spirit" (v. 20)

A grounded believer *is* more than a convert! He is like a trained teller distinguishing counterfeit money from the real thing. Being more than a convert is the result of continuous repetition of ingesting the Word then obeying it. *"Abide in me and my words abide in you."* (John 15:7 NKJV) See Ephesians 6:1-18

Notes for Jude

Journal for the Week

A. Relational Victory

B. Relational Challenges

C. Personal Victories

    a. Overcoming hidden sin or sin harmful to a family member or a friend.

    b. Bad Habit diminished, good one either started or sustained.

D. Personal Challenges

As the rain and the snow

come down from heaven,

and so not return to it

without watering the earth

and making it bud and flourish,

so that it yields seed for the sower

and bread for the eater,

so is my word that goes out

from my mouth;

It will not return to me empty,

but will accomplish what I desire

and achieve the purpose for

which I sent it.

Isaiah 55:10-11

Blessed are they who wash their robes

That they may have the right

To the tree of life.

And may go through the gates

Into the city.

I am the Alpha and the Omega

The First and the Last

The Beginning and the End.

CONCLUDING DISERTATION

Worship Wars

A reading of the second and third chapters of Revelation tells us the ideal church of that early period was difficult to find. Some say these two chapters were imagery, representative of the progression of the Church over the centuries. Whatever the case, all of the inspired writers of the New Testament make it apparent, worship wars were a part of the early church. In that time, it was circumcision and uncircumcision. Today, its liturgy in general and music in particular. There has always been division over immersion verses sprinkling and more recently women in the ministry and same-sex-marriage. With the advent of rock and roll in the mid twentieth century, it was only a matter of time hymnals and choir robes would be replaced with drums and guitars. It is hard to imagine any church carting off their hymnals to be boxed up in the basement. But that is exactly what many churches did.

Hymnals and choir robes were products <u>designed by their makers for worship</u> and specifically, <u>for the glory of God</u>. Rock and roll was designed for the world and to glorify man, specifically, the icons of the genre. The two were destined to clash as rock music and its cousins began appearing in many if not most church worship services. The result split many congregations and was responsible for pastoral appointments as well as dismissals. Certainly the devil had his way in these instances. There is no denying this!

Anyone grounded in fertile soil knows <u>the world's culture in no way glorifies God</u>. We also point out the designers of hymnals and robes had only God in mind. It is significant to remember, the hymnal and robe genre didn't birth an idol worship culture or put anyone into drug rehab or worse, kill them! Are we saying here that pop styled worship music and its various cousins ought to be expeditiously expelled from the Church? We are saying, based on Romans 12:2, 1 John 2:15 and Ezekiel 28-13, <u>be sure the Spirit moving inside you</u> is from above and not from the stage to the front.

We must fastidiously consider the Congregational Body. Worship is not a spectator sport! If we attend a church that never <u>gives us opportunity to sing</u>, we are being denied the opportunity to practice for the singing we will personally do in Heaven. We should therefore, run out the door of any spectator church and never look back. Looking back might turn us into a pillar of salt. (Genesis 19:26)

Busyness

"As Jesus and his disciples were on their way, he came to a village where a woman named Martha opened her home to him. She had a sister called <u>Mary, who sat at the Lord's feet listening</u> to what he said. But <u>Martha was distracted</u> by all the preparations that had to be made. She came to him and asked, Lord, don't you care that my sister has left me to do the work by myself? Tell her to help me!"

"Martha, Martha, the Lord answered, you are worried and upset about many things, but only one thing is needed. Mary has chosen what is better."

Luke 10:38-40, 41-41

If Satan can't corrupt us, he will make us busy. He can make one's sundry list of obligations a source of pride and self-worth. Excessive busyness can give people a feeling of <u>elevated status</u>. Saying to friends, "Let me check my schedule and see if I can work you in," is cold, prideful and demeans them. It is tacit bragging of our importance. Unwittingly, it is a form of idol worship. And the idol is self!

Our Lord never had need to check his schedule to see if He could work somebody in! I am sorry to burst the bubble of some of our perhaps more affluent and busy believers who delight in hectic networking. An overfilled calendar is useless worldliness. And when our busyness puffs us up, the devil truly has a grip on our throats. There is even danger of believing we are saved when indeed we are still lost.

Are we saying we shouldn't commit to scheduled activities? <u>We are saying it is pompous to flaunt our schedule</u>. We are saying, leave yourself quiet time, some wiggle room if you will. We don't always have to be constantly engaged with somebody, at some place, even for good, or <u>with a communicative device</u>.

Let us never be too busy to spend a few minutes with the Lord reading His word or praying for one in need? *"Be still."* (Psalm 46:10) When the devil fails to corrupt us, he is ever so delighted when he keeps us too busy to commune with our Lord. <u>Communion with the Lord is the consummation of our relationship with Christ.</u>

In our house is another Mary. Aside from Sunday when we attend church, this Mary sets aside a time each morning for Bible reading and study. Our conversations afterward generally include what she discovered about God and about herself. Very often our conversations aide my lesson preparations. For us, Scripture is part of our everyday chit-chat. Oh yes, this other Mary is my wife to whom this book is applicably dedicated.

Don't Squander an Opportunity to do Something

What should we do when we find ourselves in the position to help someone? The Scripture is clear, help them! How tragic for our society when time after time dozens die in one single mass shooting event and the best members of Congress can do is stand and observe a minute of silence! Did Rahab observe a minute of silence when the two spies needed help? Did Esther observe a minute of silence when her people needed her help? With the fall in the Garden of Eden, did heaven observe a minute of silence when men, including members of Congress, needed God's help?

Apparently, perversion of the Second Amendment has replaced the Parable of the Good Samaritan in the minds of some. How hypocritical to protect the unborn and then do nothing to protect them after they see the light of day. Scores of children are murdered in a hail of bullets fired from a weapon of war and the most those who can do something about this is observe a minute of silence? How feeble to change the subject to mental health. How calloused to voice; "We can't stop them all so we will do nothing!" Beloved, *you will know them by their fruit.*

Praise be to Baylor University Board of Regents in Waco, Texas. When young women were being assaulted, they didn't just observe a minute of silence. They acted! They didn't simply think we can't change human nature so we will do nothing. They took steps to protect young women charged to their care. Can elected officials do any less? Let us praise those who help others and expose those who are only interested in helping their reelection!

Suffering

The trials of life come in many forms and from many sources. Some are self-inflicted by poor choices. Others are a result of slanderous tongues against us. And some trials are a result of the neglect of others. The beneficial trials come from the Lord. These are the ones designed with one purpose in mind, to draw us closer unto Himself.

> *"Consider it pure joy, my brothers,*
> *whenever you face trials of many kinds."*
> **James 1:2**

How many run to the Lord crying for mercy after winning a new car, or are given box seats to watch their favorite sports team? The best we might hear for receiving something significant is *God is good!* But is God not as good when we don't win? Beloved, <u>God is at His best when we cry for mercy</u>. Our God is not a God of *goodies*, He is a God of Mercy.

Lazarus was sick. *"When he heard this, Jesus said, "This sickness will not end in death. No, it is for God's glory so that God's Son may be glorified through it."* (John 11:4) Lazarus died! It would be four days before Jesus came. By then the body emitted the odor of death. Lazarus' two sisters were very upset because to them, Jesus took His sweet time in coming to save him. One of the great lessons of this story is this. <u>Time does not control God. God controls time!</u> Jesus raised up Lazarus in His time. God is more interested in firming our Faith than granting reprieve from difficulty.

The problem of the two sisters is the same many have today, focus! This is what the Scriptures are talking about when the word maturity comes up. We <u>are attuned to this world rather than the one to come</u>. We have difficulty understanding God's time. The more difficult the task, the more Christ is glorified when it is solved! Redeeming you and me is the most difficult thing God has ever done. For who among us is worthy to save unto being with our Lord? Yet Revelation 21:3 promises exactly that. When trials come, one of two emotions is produced, hope or despair! When cancer is announced, what is the hope of a Christian? Of course a quick and painless cure is wished for. But <u>our hope is in the knowledge of knowing</u> if this thing kills us, we have no doubt of our deliverance into the presence of the Lord. This is a mature faith.

A trial may not be life threatening but still, <u>our focus has to be on the world to come</u>. Even if we don't have a fatal disease, we, along with all the world are going to die.

If we read Hebrews 11, many of God's people did experience triumph in this physical world, but many did not. (Hebrews 11:35-39) The Death and Resurrection of Jesus had absolutely nothing to do with triumphing over our circumstances and everything to do with triumphing over *all* that is dying. For those in Hebrews 11 who didn't triumph over their circumstances, *"God had planned something better."* (Hebrews 11:40)

Whatever the trial before us, God put it there to strengthen our resolve to endure until He comes for us. Reprieve is one thing, deliverance is entirely a different subject. The mature understand this and will <u>remain faithful until the time of their deliverance</u>. When He tests our Faith, He observes to whom we seek relief.

We may not be dying from our present trial, but there is <u>one coming when we do</u>. Not one will survive the limits God has placed on the flesh. Even the folks we see working out in the gym three times a week or getting up early to run some miles will die from something. These truths are not meant to be negative or to frighten, but to *rejoice* when God sends us tribulations so great, we are compelled to cry for mercy!

> *"The righteous cry out, and the Lord hears them;*
> *He delivers them from all their troubles."*
>
> **Psalm 34:17**